ARCHITECTURE
FOR ◆ THE ◆ GODS

ARCHITECTURE
FOR ◆ THE ◆ GODS

MICHAEL J. CROSBIE

DEDICATION:

To the people of St. John's Episcopal Church,
Essex, Connecticut

First published in Australia in 1999 by
The Images Publishing Group Pty Ltd
ACN 059 734 431
6 Bastow Place, Mulgrave, Victoria 3170, Australia
Telephone: +(61 3) 9561 5544 Facsimile: +(61 3) 9561 4860
E-mail: books@images.com.au

National Library of Australia Cataloguing-in-Publication Data

Crosbie, Michael J.
Architecture for the Gods.

ISBN 1 86470 005 X.

1. Church buildings – Pictorial works. 2. Church architecture –
Pictorial works. I. Title.

726.5

Designed by The Graphic Image Studio Pty Ltd
Mulgrave, Australia

Printed by Everbest Printing, Hong Kong

PREFACE

This compendium of recent religious architecture in the Americas appears at first to have no unifying theme, except for the fact (of course) that this architecture is for the gods. There is certainly no agreement on style: in here you will find a bit of everything—Traditional, Historicist, Classical, Modern, and everything that has come after Modern, and is still coming. The gods, it appears, are much more relaxed about the sanctity of a proper style than your average architect is.

Architectural creativity in religious buildings is quite vibrant. Here we find many examples of new patterns of worship space, experiments in the architecture of the sacred. Unlike any other public building—town hall, factory, corporate office, or school—it is possible that the design of religious architecture offers generous latitude. The secular buildings mentioned above must conform to certain standards of function. But the religious building does not. Certainly, there are expectations of what a church, synagogue, or mosque should look like. A certain scale—one to make us feel humble in the presence of the Divine—is nearly always present. Materials such as stained glass and stone almost automatically suggest a house of worship. An assemblage of materials and space that draws our eyes upward, away from earthly pursuits, is often found.

Given these 'givens,' departures from them abound among the projects in these pages. In certain ways, these are the buildings that are most exciting, because they fashion sacred places where we might not expect to find them, with materials and space that challenge old ideas. These religious structures are testament not only to their creative designers (who are usually not squeamish about challenging tradition) but to the congregations and clergy who give their consent to experiment. Great sacred architecture is always a collaboration.

The unifying theme, then, might be that even after thousands of years, religious buildings continue to be wide open to interpretation. Evolution, experimentation, challenges to tradition, the invention of new identities —all of these qualities can be found in religious buildings that we design and build today.

Michael J. Crosbie

CONTENTS

Architecture for the Gods

INTRODUCTION

By Fr. Richard S. Vosko, Ph.D.

The 1997 United States Census report indicates that US$6 billion was spent on construction and renovation of religious building in that year. Further according to the F.W. Dodge research unit, 'new religious construction last year (1997) reached its highest level in three decades—41 billion square feet.' These numbers may not sound like a lot when you compare them to the budgets and sizes of non-religious projects. However, when you consider that the members of the congregations are providing the funding, it becomes quite a remarkable phenomenon in this era. Why this burst of growth?

Enthusiasm surrounding the new millennium, shifting populations, and changes in spiritual attitudes are some of the reasons for the religious building boom. History suggests that times of transition, such as moving into a new century, are often accompanied by an atmosphere of uncertainty that can foster a renewed search for the sacred. Many people return to religion hoping to find a sense of security and peace of mind. The organization of new religions and the reforms of mainstream religions create a rise in membership rolls and, thus, the need for larger or newer houses of worship.

Much of the construction of new religious spaces is taking place in the south or southwest part of the US. This is caused in part by shifting populations and new immigration paths. As the baby boomers of World War II retire early they appear to be moving to warmer climates and away from the northern industrial centers. Also, the numbers of immigrants now coming to North America from Asia, Latin America, and the Caribbean far surpass those who come from Eastern and Western Europe. They too seem to settle in the south. Together these factors contribute to the need for new houses of worship that reflect the religious traditions of multi-cultural populations.

What do these religious buildings look like? A recent article in the *Wall Street Journal* quoted diverse insights to support one design or another. The range of architectural styles covers a broad spectrum. At one end there is the functional warehouse church devoid of any religious symbols. At the other end there is the exact replica of a house of worship built in another country in another age. Somewhere in between there are nondescript religious buildings considered to be either in the vanguard of contemporary design or destined to fail as a work of architecture altogether.

There appears to be no dominant style of religious architecture in the Americas. Therefore, one wonders about the factors contributing to such a diverse palette of sacred spaces. By way of introduction to Dr Michael J. Crosbie's fine compendium of recent worship spaces I would like to identify and describe just a few factors which I believe are affecting the design of religious buildings.

Still reeling from the reactions to Modernism (Post-Modernism, Neo-Vernacular, Neo-Classicism, and High-Tech or Late Modern) many congregations are looking for spaces that are both more stimulating and, in some ways, familiar. Therefore, the 'anything goes' architectural plan is no longer a satisfying template for most houses of prayer.

For some religions the greatest influence today appears to be rooted in the recovery of the time honored components of sacred spaces. A new appreciation for scale, light, color, and texture now serve as building blocks for designing religious edifices. These ingredients conjure up images of soaring cathedrals like Notre Dame in Chartres or the Moorish flair of the Temple Maggiore in Florence. Further, the creation of pathways, portals, and centers are reminiscent of the well-known sacred sites of old, whether it be the ceremonial complex at Tiahuanaco in the Altiplano of Bolivia or the curious Neolithic passage tomb at Newgrange in County Meath, Ireland.

In other words architects, designers, and congregations are searching for ways to 'capture' a sense of the sacred in their buildings. While the appearance of flying buttresses and gargoyles may be relics of a bygone era, advanced technology in all of the building trades has made it possible to utilize new materials and structural systems to create forms that are just as spiritually rewarding. Some less imaginative designers and architects may have retreated to the history books for ideas that would appeal to congregations. But other, more innovative professionals have taken up the challenge and have moved into the cutting edge of religious architecture by respecting time-honored examples of worship spaces but rendering new ones in a more courageous fashion.

The results are appealing. Many new worship spaces now have labyrinthine pathways leading to great portals inspired by mythological definition. The interiors are graced by high ceilings, ample natural light, and seating configurations that draw worshipers into the liturgical activity not as spectators but partners in the ritual dance. Dr Crosbie identifies new churches, synagogues, and mosques that are perfect examples of this creative effort.

This movement should not be interpreted, however, as a disregard for the past. In fact, just the opposite is true on the American scene. While the historic preservation of significant sites and spaces is accompanied by an ongoing struggle for funding there is a renewed interest in saving grand old religious buildings. The passion for maintaining this architectural heritage bequeathed by the first religious communities is feverish. In fact, new life is being breathed into many spaces that have become old and wrinkled because of dying neighborhoods. The slow return to the central city by those who are fleeing the ennui of exurbia has resulted in new pilgrims searching for a place to go for Sabbat Services or Sunday Mass. Again, Dr Crosbie cites a couple of sacred spaces that have been beautifully restored and, in some instances, reorganized to accommodate ritual reforms.

Another reason for the new look in many worship spaces has to do with liturgical reform. Traditionally, religious buildings are primarily constructed to house the rituals and ceremonies of the congregation. While some faith communities cling steadfastly to ancestral rites others have embarked on liturgical reforms that have altered their worship practice in very noticeable ways.

One example is the impact of the Second Vatican Council on the liturgical life of the Roman Catholic Church. Where once the liturgy was thought to be conducted by the clergy for the people, now worship, it is generally believed, is an act of the whole congregation. Therefore, the interiors of churches have been designed or rearranged to accommodate more active and conscious participation in the rites by both the clergy and laity. To facilitate this ritual reform, where possible, the altar is no longer located at one end of a long nave. Instead, the table is now placed more in the midst of the congregation thereby creating a more intimate and engaging worship experience. Other Christian denominations and some Jewish movements have shown similar developments in their rituals causing the reorganization of their worship spaces, such as moving the pulpit or bimah more into the congregation.

Liturgical reform and the new look of houses of prayer to accommodate the changes have created a concern for some members of different faiths. The respect for tradition, the love of older worship spaces, and the realization that such buildings can never again be replicated in the same way is at the heart of the anguish. This anxiety is a touchstone for my last and perhaps most important factor in the design of worship environments memory.

I am convinced that a worship space by its nature is a place of memory. When a synagogue, mosque, or church does not trigger the memory (and its cousin, imagination) the place will not serve the faithful in a transformative way. Like the religious rituals they house, sacred spaces are arenas where life cycles are celebrated and remembered. They are places that help people disengage momentarily from ordinary everyday life. They make it possible to enter the realm of the mystical or extraordinary world. While many people journey to mountains, deserts, or oceans for spiritual refreshment others find solace and encouragement in their houses of prayer.

James Ingo Freed once remarked to me that he designed the Holocaust Memorial Museum to be a 'resonator.' The purpose of the Memorial, he said, is to play back the memory of the horrible reality of the Holocaust. In many ways, that is the purpose of religious architecture. On one hand worship spaces are crucibles of memories. On the other hand, they can help the worshiper imagine how things might be. This combination of memory and imagination can help some people survive. It is one of the ingredients of religious ritual even in traditions that typically do not use ceremonies in their gatherings. The very act of a community coming together to pray, to listen to sacred texts and sermons, to sing hymns or engage in a communal meal is for many a source of sustenance.

Therefore, religious buildings cannot be thought of as mere containers for ritual objects and activity. I am certain that they are metaphors. They are extensions of the religious experience. They derive meaning from the faith and the traditions of the congregation and they nourish the same community to grow and develop into new generations of believers. Worship spaces can be resonators when the stories of the faith community are apparent in the very design of the building. The use of color, light, scale, and art, as well as the incorporation of pathways, portals, and centers can contribute to the religious experience. The worship space is a story-book of old tales and many chapters still unwritten.

There are many religious traditions that do not attach such metaphorical significance to their houses of prayer. Nevertheless, it is safe to say that most people who belong to a faith tradition are searching for some kind of experience that will move them toward a better way of life. A life that is, in some way, holy and wholly other than what is being experienced now. This is the tremendous burden placed on religious architecture—to serve as a firm foundation of faith and a platform for courage and creativity.

There are other factors that are probably equally important to some readers of this fine book. Context or regionalism should not be overlooked. How a building fits into and contributes to the neighborhood aesthetic, whether it is the edge of a desert or a noisy city street, is important. And, certainly, the issues surrounding ecology can not be forgotten. Perhaps the wake-up call sounding the pressing issues affecting the environment has not yet stirred the hearts or minds of the design community. The use of recycled materials, active solar systems, waste reduction systems, straw bale walls, etc. is beginning to re-emerge as a certifiable approach to the design and construction of many buildings. One can imagine that the religious community should take this opportunity to model a respect for the environment by exploring ingenuous ways to construct worship spaces.

Dr Crosbie, architect and scholar, has done a great service by compiling this compendium of significant religious buildings. As you enjoy the photographs and descriptions my hope is that this book will serve as a treasured record of the traditions and foundations as well as the visions and creative energies exemplified by religious architecture.

PROJECTS

ST. JAMES EPISCOPAL CHURCH

Fairhope, Alabama, USA

This new church at Fairhope, Alabama, serves the expanding population of the Eastern Shore of Mobile Bay. The aspirations of the congregation and vestry were to construct a church that referred to regional traditions of Gulf Coast carpenter Gothic structures. The design by Errol Barron/Michael Toups Architects looks new and old at the same time. The interior of the church has specific references to its structure and organization, which are modern, but the lancet windows and arches at the side aisles, for example, are not in any way autonomous architectural elements. There is an overt attempt to work within a style.

The site is a 10-acre hill at the entrance to Fairhope, zoned as green space except for the church, which will be surrounded by trees. The building is sited so that the 80-foot-high steeple is seen as one approaches along Scenic Highway 98 from the west (from Mobile). The other buildings—parish hall, school, and chapel—are concealed behind the church from this approach. The group of structures (except the classroom wing) are sited around a lawn or garth edged by covered walkways and porches. After-church functions, held in the parish hall, open out to the garth. The offices are placed closest to the parking, the bulk of which is behind the buildings and screened by trees.

1 *Inspired by Gothic tradition, the exterior is spare and comforting*
2 *Sketch*
3 *Site plan*

1

2

The buildings are all sheathed in clear heart redwood board and batten siding, the porches are constructed of mahogany, and all the wood is painted bone white. The structure of the main nave is a simple framing scheme of rafters and collar beams supported by brackets which give an arched shape to the space when seen along the main axis of the sanctuary. Chandeliers, designed and stenciled by the architects, display the symbols of St. James—shells, scrolls, and staffs.

The spatial organization does not follow recent efforts to cluster seating around the altar, but refers instead to tradition of the center aisle. The choir loft, located over the entry of the church, has a double staircase to accommodate the double procession for services favored at St. James.

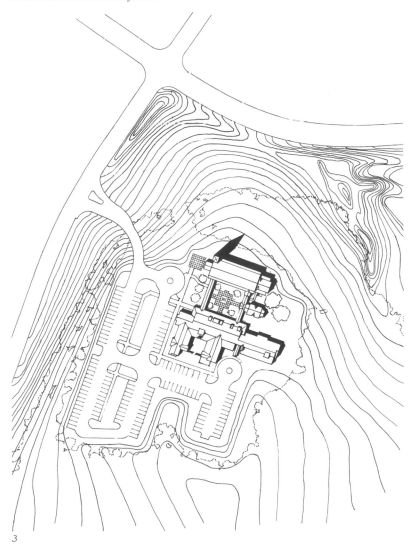

3

4 *View across courtyard towards chapel*
5 *Building plan*
6 *Church interior incorporates elegant details*
   inspired by Gothic tradition
Following pages:
7 *Sanctuary is a refuge of light and space*
8 *Central nave of chapel is an intimate space*
Photography: Alan Karchmer

4

5

6

7

ABBEY CHURCH OF ST. BENOIT

St-Benoit-du-Lac, Quebec, Canada

This church for the Benedictine monastery of St-Benoit-du-Lac, designed by Dan S. Hanganu, Architect, is the third edifice at the monastery, following those of the cloister and refectory from the late-1930s, and the hostel and the church foundations dating from the late-1950s. The design springs from the original concept for the church, building upon the existing foundation and elaborating the volumetric idea of a proposed section. This intervention respects the architectural context, enriching the ensemble.

The church is ordered by the specific liturgical requirements of monastic life. The sanctuary and the altar become the central focus of the space towards which architectural lines converge, and upon which natural light concentrates. A horizontal progression culminates in the verticality of a large rectangular tower from which overhead natural light showers stainless steel cables placed directly above the altar. The constantly changing diffused light, captured and transformed within this space, evokes the ethereal qualities of meditation and spiritual uplift.

The structure, an assemblage of metallic elements, springs from the existing concrete arches and columns. The steel columns disengage and soar upwards to form the roof's pointed arches, with an airiness suggested by traditional flying buttresses.

Continued

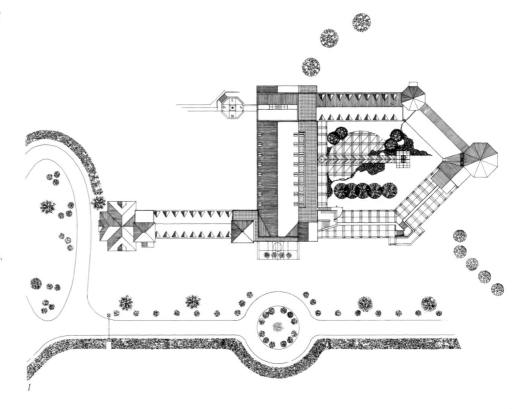

1

2

1   Site plan
2   The Abbey Church as it appears in the hilly landscape of St-Benoit-du-Lac
Opposite:
    New Abbey Church is lighter in color, and connects to existing bell tower to left and cloister at right

The interior forms emphasize simplicity, serenity, and a search for timeless imagery, symbolic of strength and continuity—all appropriate for a place of worship. The exterior, clad in granite, clearly expresses the organization of the interior. The principal facade is extended vertically by a narrow bridge evocative of traditional monastic architecture, which connects the existing tower and its lookout to the north with a new tower to the south. The bridge allows the ritual of the monastic walk to be enhanced by contemplation of the surrounding landscape. Placed between the church and the courtyard, a cloister connects the existing monks' cells with the atrium of the church. Above, a linear exterior terrace restates the idea of the monachal walk. The church portico, surmounted by a rose window symbolizing the *Tree of Life,* welcomes all worshipers.

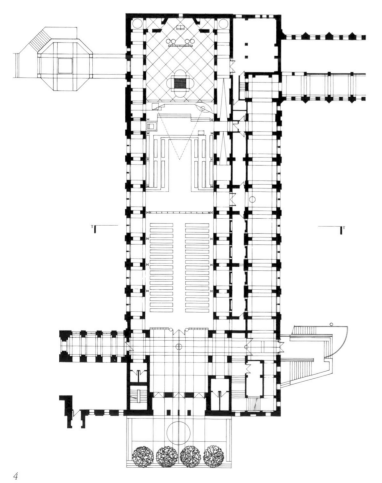

4

5

4 Floor plan
5 Entry from the narthex to the nave, with the
   sanctuary beyond
6 Chapel and staircase anchor the corner of the
   church and reveal its transparency

6

7

7 Light enters the sanctuary and grazes the
   unadorned brick walls
8 The nave is accented with vertical elements,
   with materials left in the natural state
9 View through the naturally lit triforium,
   which overlooks the nave
10 Above the nave and sanctuary, light enters
   the triforium through skylights
Photography: Alan Karchmer

8

9

10

TEMPLE JEREMIAH GOLDER CHAPEL

Northfield, Illinois, USA

This intimate chapel is a new addition to an existing synagogue. Designed by H. Gary Frank Architects, the chapel accommodates 125 people and is the perfect setting for small weddings, bar and bat mizvahs, children's services, funerals, lectures, and concerts.

The new chapel is located in a southwest corner of the existing building, just off its lobby. The exterior of the chapel is designed in deference to the original building's austere brick walls. The cultural concerns of this project were the driving force behind the design. The gently angled, curved, and stepped walls and ceilings are not only designed to enhance the acoustics by minimizing echo and reverberation, but also to create a visual hierarchy within the space.

The central focus of the chapel is the bimah wall, within which the ark is housed. Made from rustic, split-faced Kasota stone and catching the glancing sun from above, this wall serves as a

reminder not only of the thousands of years that Jews have struggled within the sands and stones of the Middle East, but also as a contemporary reminder of the Western Wall in Jerusalem. The same material is used on the floor, which gives it a time-worn quality.

The chapel's other three walls and the ceilings are designed to be understated, with naturally finished materials, allowing the focus points to be the bimah wall, the eternal light, and soft natural light coming from a concealed source above. Seating is arranged on three sides of the bimah which extends into the space. This design emphasizes the chapel's intimate nature and allows congregants to see each other. The pews, the fanciful ark for the torah scrolls, the eternal light, and the lectern are designed by Dakota Jackson to be in harmony with Frank's architecture.

1

2

1 The chapel is an intimate space, with the bimah appearing as a stage-set for worship
2 Detail of the ark opening, with the delicate eternal light playing off the textured masonry wall surface
3 Chapel pews, table, and other sanctuary furniture are designed by Dakota Jackson in the spirit of architecture
4 The ark emerges from the rustic stone wall, protected by a canopy, and lighted indirectly

Photography: James Yocum

3

4

FIRST CHURCH OF CHRIST, SCIENTIST

Glendale, California, USA

Two Christian Science congregations in a small, prosperous Southern California town united to build a new church on a small site, which made accommodation of program and parking requirements a challenge.

Moore Ruble Yudell Architects' approach groups the various uses around a courtyard. The main auditorium, Sunday School building, offices, and meeting rooms are all entered through it, and arrival from the parking areas on two levels is at one corner, marked by a tower that brings light down a stairwell to the lower level. Ancillary meeting rooms and offices complete the enclosure of the courtyard on three sides, while on the fourth broad steps and a ramp open out to the street.

The courtyard works as the outdoor heart of the church, encouraging informal gatherings. The entrance to the foyer of the auditorium is at the courtyard's opposite corner, extending the sequence of movement to it. The foyer itself is a glassy bay that brings the courtyard in and creates, in the evening, a glowing pavilion of light along the street.

The auditorium, seating 250, is filled with filtered clerestory light and offers views to two small gardens, protected by generous gables. The space's large openings recall the Arts and Crafts' tradition of the region's architectural heritage. The central aisle of the auditorium runs on the diagonal, increasing the sense of spaciousness and focussing attention on the reader's podium. The wall behind the podium is subtly colored, washed with sunlight from a hidden skylight. Wood latticework further articulates the focus of the room, extending to screen the pipes of the organ.

The Arts and Crafts' tradition evoked by the design of the church is realized in simple materials. Walls are painted board and batten, roofs are composition shingle. A small site and limited budget have not hindered the creation of a tranquil, memorable church that is responsive to its place, its tradition, and its congregation.

1

2

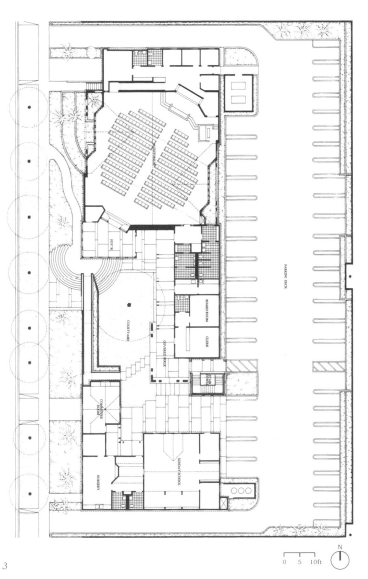

3

1 View from the west, as the church faces the street,
  with sanctuary to the left
2 Elevation
3 Floor plan

4   The glassy foyer of the sanctuary overlooks the
    sunny courtyard
5   The stair tower dominates the small courtyard,
    which is the heart of the complex
Following pages:
    The auditorium is a light-filled space, with
    a diagonal center aisle.
Photography: Timothy Hursley

4

5

GOOD SHEPHERD CATHOLIC CHURCH

Miami, Florida, USA

Located on an eight-acre site in a typical Miami suburb, this new church has a central plaza that is defined by the church, two existing parish buildings, and a future school. A tower marks the main entry into the church and is the focus of the plaza. The 25,800-square-foot new church and office complex was designed by Duany Plater-Zyberk & Company and built within a very limited budget of about US$2 million. Consequently, the building derives its aesthetics from the proportion of its spaces, openings, and structural elements, rather than applied ornament.

The plan addresses two conflicting parish perspectives regarding worship spaces, a liturgical dichotomy present in the modern Catholic Church. One contingent wanted a church with a tall, linear, and symmetrical nave and the altar at one end. The other faction wanted a post-Vatican II space that seated the congregation around the altar to encourage greater participation. The resolution of these two contrary directives yielded the two principal spaces: a traditional long, tall, and narrow narthex with the entry tower at one end and the

Continued

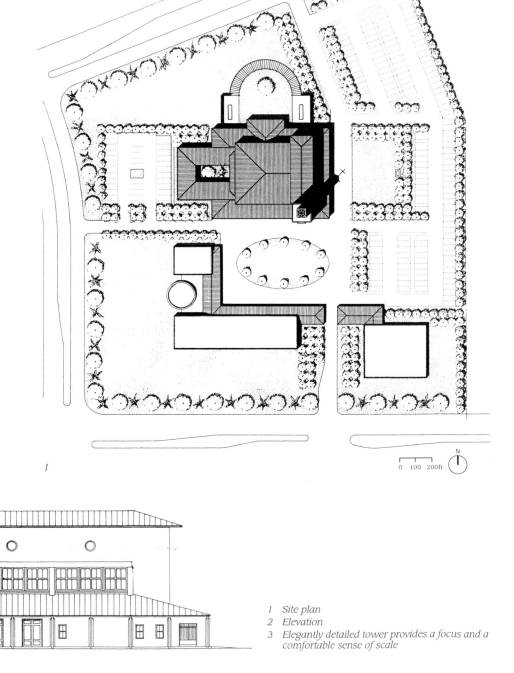

1

2

1   Site plan
2   Elevation
3   Elegantly detailed tower provides a focus and a
    comfortable sense of scale

3

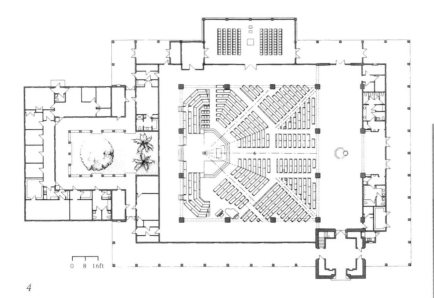

4

baptismal font at its center; and a square nave containing an altar that is almost completely surrounded by the assembly, the choir, and the presider.

Numerological symbolism structures the spaces, from the basic 7-foot planning module, to the 12 columns demarcating the nave and representing the original 12 apostles.

Given the programmatic request for a bright interior filled with natural light, passive solar techniques were used to minimize heat load as well as the need for excessive air conditioning. The main assembly space, which is ringed with a continuous set of clerestory windows, is protected with an overhang of 7 feet that keeps out direct sunlight for most of the day. A portico surrounding the entire perimeter of the church, and connecting to the office cloister in the rear, also shields the gathering spaces from daytime heat gain. In the assembly spaces, the nave, and the narthex, the air conditioning vents and the sound amplification speakers are concealed behind a triforium of perforated and louvered metal panels beneath the tall clerestories.

5

4   Floor plan
5   The loggia provides welcome shade in this hot, humid climate
6   East side expresses the volume of the sanctuary with its clerestory windows
7   Sanctuary space is large, open, and airy, with abundant natural light
Following pages:
    Seating in the sanctuary congregates around the altar in participatory fashion
Photography: Carlos Morales

6

7

ST. ANDREW PRESBYTERIAN CHURCH

Sonoma, California, USA

On Palm Sunday 1989, a fire destroyed the carriage house in rural Sonoma County that had been converted to house St. Andrew Presbyterian Church. Shortly after, Turnbull Griffin & Haesloop Architects was hired to design a new church facility including sanctuary, fellowship hall, classrooms, and offices. The architect's intention was to recapture the special quality of the lost building while better accommodating the church's needs.

The site is a gently sloping six-acre parcel with a winter creek cutting diagonally across. The new church is a large barn-like structure topped by a high cupola. The cupola admits a flood of natural light into the central octagonal narthex, which opens onto the sanctuary and the fellowship hall, allowing all three spaces to open onto one another for special occasions. Classrooms are located in a one-story wing enclosing the entry courtyard.

Both Mary Griffin and William Turnbull, Jr., the designers, were raised knowing Presbyterian houses of worship and wanted St. Andrew to recall the austere simplicity of older churches, while making the space feel inclusive and welcoming. The chancel has indirect natural light creating a soft glow on the wall featuring the cross. Corner windows open out onto views of the surrounding fields.

In keeping with the traditional agricultural buildings in this region, as well as many Presbyterian churches, this church is constructed of wood. The exterior is plywood with battens, painted white. The interior includes wooden trusses, rafters, and decking. This new building fits comfortably into the site, while meeting the varied needs of a growing congregation. The building was awarded an American Wood Council Honor Award as well as a national Honor Award from the American Institute of Architects.

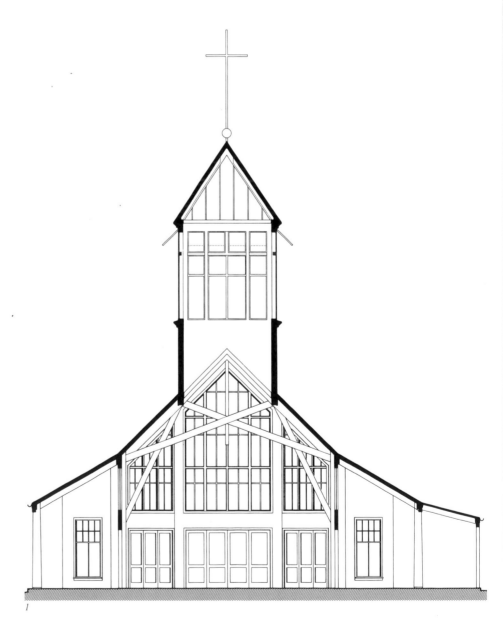

1

1 Elevation
2 East elevation modulates siding pattern with cross pattern, and offers a small porch off the fellowship hall
3 Site plan
4 The church's architecture is inspired by the rural farm buildings in this part of California

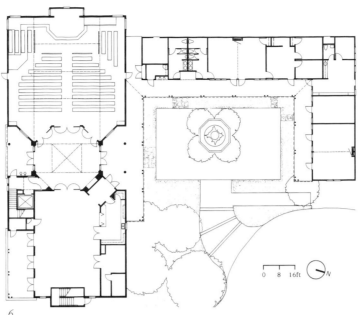

Opposite:
    View from the octagonal narthex space into the sanctuary, with trusses overhead

6   *Floor plan*

7   *The stark exterior is balanced with an elegant simplicity in the sanctuary, with a board and batten motif*

Photography: Mark Darley/Esto Photographics

0   8   16ft

6

7

NORTH SHORE SYNAGOGUE

Kings Point, New York, USA

An addition to an existing Hebrew academy, this synagogue designed by Alexander Gorlin Architect fills the corner of two classroom wings. Most of the building's form is buried, as zoning set a height limit of 45 feet above sea level on a site where the entrance is at 27 feet. Light enters the sanctuary from above through strips of clerestory windows on the periphery and a large glass cube over the ark. This cube of light is fractured by two inverted triangles that evoke not only the Star of David, but also the 'emanations of the sefirot' and the 'breaking of the vessels' described by the kabbalah, the ancient Jewish mystical tradition.

The concept of the stained glass in the sanctuary derives from the tradition of assigning different colors to the light of the emanations of the sefirot. The window glass is lightly colored so as to allow a view out to the surrounding trees. Each day is represented by a modulation of the

Continued

1

2

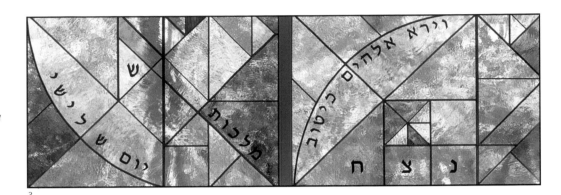

1   Entrance to the synagogue, which fills a
    corner of an existing Hebrew academy
2   Despite being partially buried, the
    synagogue interior is filled with light
3   Detail of the stained glass windows,
    which contain Judaic symbols and
    simple geometry

3

4&5 *Development of abstract Judaic symbol*
  6 *Axial view of the sanctuary and Ark with large door in closing position*
7&8 *Development of abstract Judaic symbol*

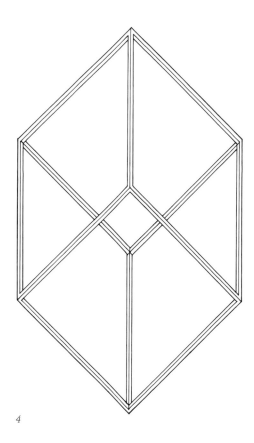

4

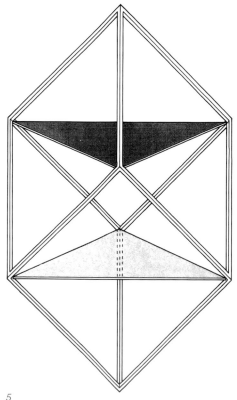

5

6

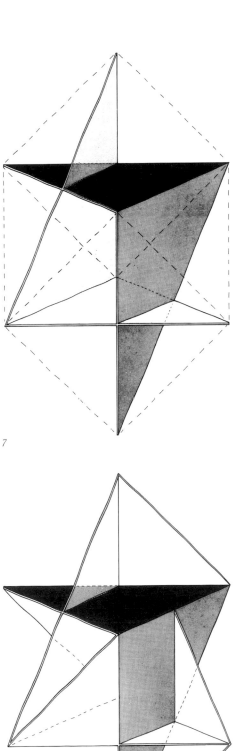

7

8

geometry and color to reflect the creation of light, vegetation, the sun, moon and stars, of animals, man and woman.

Breaking open the corner of the space is the cubic frame of the ark inscribed by two inverted triangles of translucent and clear glass. Light emerges from the square opening above and extends out to the edges of the interior of the space. The inverted triangles reflect not only light, but sound as well, as the cantor (ritual chanter) faces the ark during services and his voice reflects back into the congregation.

Upon opening the doors to the ark, a ritual curtain (parochet) covers the torah within. The design is a diagram of the pattern of the sefirot and their Hebrew names. Large bronze doors close the ark, and are inscribed with 12 squares representing the original number of the Tribes of Israel, and 12 rectangles to represent the Diaspora of the Jewish people after the destruction of the Temple in Jerusalem.

9

10

11

11   Clerestory windows in the roof of the
      synagogue deliver soft, colored, natural
      light
12   A variety of colors give the natural light
      depth and interest
Photography: Peter Aaron/ESTO

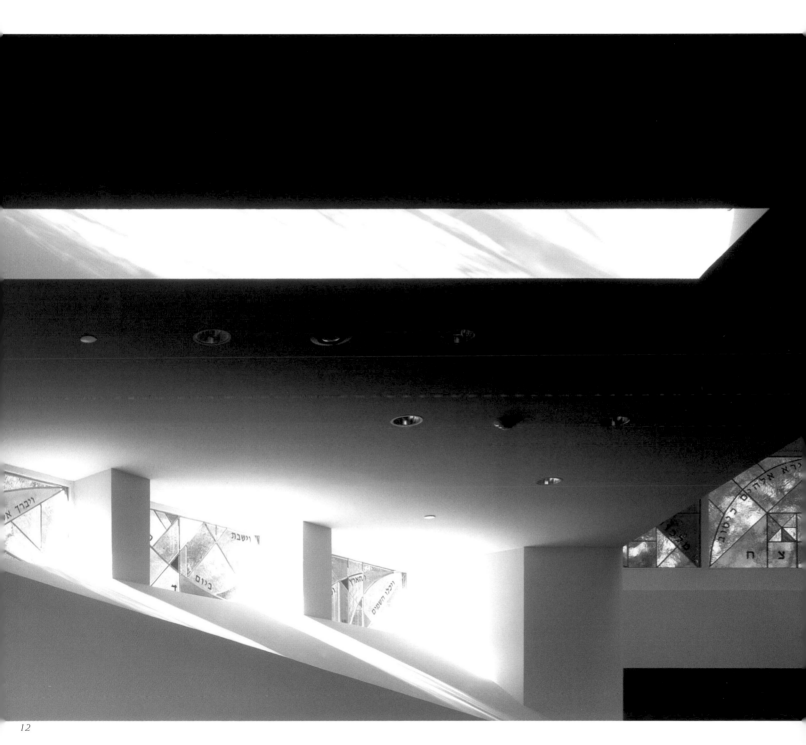

12

UNITARIAN FELLOWSHIP OF HOUSTON

Houston, Texas, USA

1

Because the values of its 150 members are humanistic rather than theistic, the Fellowship requested that this church have a distinctly human scale and use honest materials simply and creatively. The modest budget also required that the structure be minimally finished, with the focus being on the places created both inside and outside the building. The project is a joint venture of architects Val Glitsch and Natalye Appel.

The two-acre site occupies a corner at the intersection of a major commercial thoroughfare and a road that borders a neighboring residential subdivision. Large groupings of pecan and oak trees occupy the outer and central areas of the property, while a strong circle of pines provides a private focal point at the rear.

The new building contains a sanctuary for speakers and performances, an administration wing including a library and office/workrooms, and an education wing with classrooms and assembly area. Each of these areas is united through a gathering place that serves as lobby, overflow meeting space, drinking and discussion hall, and dining room.

An L-shaped courtyard scheme is created by a long metal 'barn' that houses education and administration functions, and a stucco 'shed' containing the sanctuary. The glazed gathering place, with fireplace and kitchen as symbolic centers, opens to the public at the southwest corner near the street intersection. Natural crushed-stone surface parking fits into existing perimeter trees. Future expansion will be accommodated at the north side of the courtyard, with the children's assembly area as the connecting hub.

Simple materials consist of synthetic stucco, corrugated metal, painted ribbed metal, aluminum windows, minimal wood trim, structural wood trusses and laminated wood beams, fiberglass shingle roof, and standing seam metal roof.

1 North elevation
2 A corner of the glassy sanctuary wing, which looks out to the trees
3 The building nestles comfortably into its wooded landscape
4 West elevation
5 The tall chimney also suggests a steeple for this non-traditional building

2

6 A corner fireplace in the gathering space gives this building a domestic feel
7 The entry and gathering space is intimate and welcoming

Photography: R. Greg Hursley

3

4

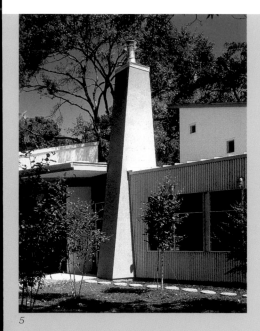

5

6

7

CHURCH OF ST. THERESE

Wilson, North Carolina, USA

Responding to this Roman Catholic congregation's desire for a church 'that looks like a church,' Gerald Allen & Jeffrey Harbinson, Architects, knew that need could be answered in traditional terms. But the resulting building had also to meet the specific requirements of contemporary Roman Catholic liturgy which, in the past 25 years, have given rise to a large variety of untraditional church designs. The site was on the main residential street of a handsome old Southern town, so the new building also had to be a good neighbor.

In order to look like a church, the building is cruciform in plan, and its windows are on the whole tall and thin. Its roof pitch is steep, and inside a critical relationship is maintained between the width of the nave and transepts and the spring-point of the sloped ceiling.

To conform to the contemporary liturgical practice, the altar is placed in the crossing, underneath the lantern and spire, with worshipers arranged on three sides. On the fourth side (the space occupied in a traditional church by the choir) stands a small daily Mass chapel. It is a building within the building, and its facade, ornamented with roses for St. Therese, and fleurs-de-lys for the Virgin Mary, provides a backdrop for the main altar.

The floor of the church is paved with brick rather than carpet (which is more usual for church flooring). This, along with the simple white walls and ceilings, is meant by the architect as a reminder of fondly remembered 18th- and early 19th-century church buildings in Virginia and in the northeastern part of North Carolina known as the Albermarle. The plain brick floors and the unadorned walls also have a spectacular effect on the acoustics, helping create an extraordinarily reverberant space ideal both for organ music and for singing. It was recently described by concert organist Carlo Curley as 'one of the finest acoustical and worship spaces in North America.'

1

1　A square lantern and spire, designed by Kent Bloomer and Kimo Griggs, sits directly above the altar
2　Site plan
3　Floor plan
4　To the left of the main facade, the building has a tower with a secondary entrance

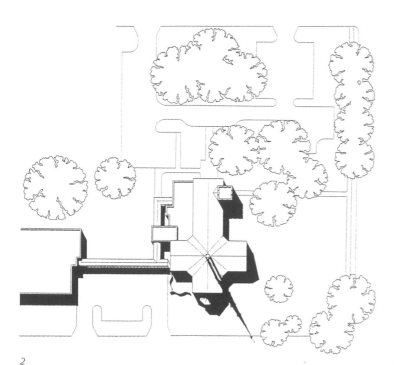

2

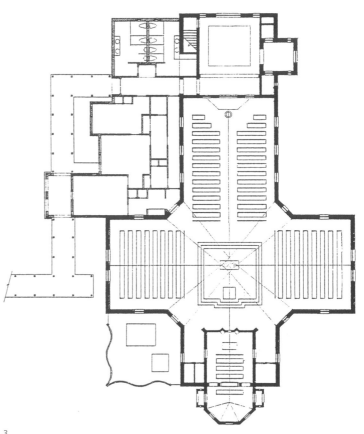

3

4

4

4 *View of the interior, showing the altar and sanctuary placed beneath the central lantern of the crossing*
5 *Presider's and concelebrants' chairs are sympathetic to the traditional design inspiration*
6 *The sanctuary is a raised brick podium with the altar, chairs, lectern, and crucifix*
Photography: Tim Buchman

5

6

GALVIN FAMILY CHAPEL

Babson College, Wellesley, Massachusetts, USA

The program for this chapel designed by William Rawn Associates was to provide a spiritual place at the heart of this New England campus. The building is almost a perfect cube. Inside, the 30-foot-high space provides a non-denominational sanctuary for gatherings of up to 50 people. The chapel has purposely been placed on the uphill side of the site to create an ascending path from the heart of the campus center that ends in a relationship between sanctuary and nature.

Exterior stone steps set flush to the sloped lawn lead up to an intimate foyer which, bathed in diffuse light, is screened from the secular world. Entering this foyer through ornamented paneled doors, the lofty sanctuary is fully revealed, with dramatic stained glass windows set against the views of the natural landscape. The walls of the building are a balance of solid and void. The two transparent walls face the uphill woods, and offer a sense of landscape, peace, and contemplation. Natural light is modulated by deciduous trees. The two solid walls are of Deer Isle granite, and face the busy central campus. These solid walls provide a sense of protection and thus solitude.

Iconography was designed to serve multiple faiths; themes of nature that are common to all religions abound in the chapel. In addition to the actual natural setting that infuses the space of the sanctuary, abstractions of nature are found in the art adorning its special features. The celestial imagery in the main doors of the sanctuary, the reeds and flowers at the base of the altar/bimah, and the dynamic waves that fill the stained glass windows—each of these serve as a reminder of man's place in the natural world. Additionally, as a nod to the spiritual reflections of the college's founder, forms derived from sailing vessels influence the hull-like ceiling of the sanctuary and the rising sail that crowns the exterior tower.

1 The sail form outside alludes to the boat-like form inside
2 The chapel is sited with windows opening to the woods uphill
3 First floor plan
4 Second floor plan
5 By night, the chapel interior glows like a gem

1

2

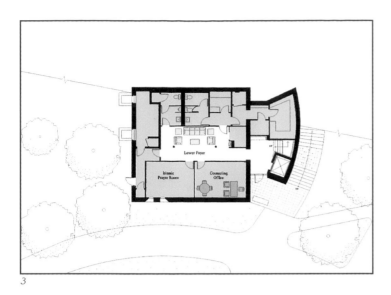

3

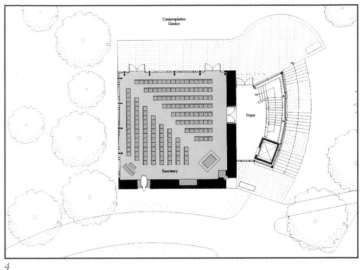

4

5

7

Previous pages:
   The boat-like form overhead suggests Christian
   imagery and the spiritual reflections of the
   college's founder
7 Chapel interior expresses the warmth of wood
   cladding two opaque walls
8 With seating oriented toward two glass walls,
   the chapel takes in the whole of nature
Photography: Steve Rosenthal

8

THE CONNELLY CHAPEL OF HOLY WISDOM

Washington Theological Union, Washington, DC., USA

This project, which encompasses building rehabilitation and new construction, is for a Roman Catholic graduate school for ministry. Its theology is based on the teachings of Vatican II, including a liturgical emphasis on the non-hierarchical assembly of persons as the focus of worship.

The seminary purchased an aging complex of buildings to become its new permanent home. Most of the seminary's needs— library, dining hall, classrooms, offices, residential rooms, etc. are accommodated in the renovated older building. KressCox Associates designed a new chapel, connected to the main building by a

glazed link passing through a small courtyard, that establishes a separate identity as the new focus for the school. Elevated above the ground on massive walls of pale yellow brick, which give way to a tracery of white metal and glass, the chapel and its bell tower act as a vertical counterpoint to the horizontal retaining wall and trellis, joining with the main building new lobby portico as a unifying foreground to the disparate background of the older buildings.

The chapel is specifically designed for the seminary's daily eucharistic liturgy, requiring two discreet but proximate zones defined by furniture placement. The singular open, neutral

space and minimal fixed furniture allow the chapel to also accommodate special ceremonial liturgies, lectures, and concerts. The chapel interior is a spare, spiritual setting that underscores the theme of light—composed of unstained maple, white plaster, and painted steel—for an assembly of up to 200 celebrants. The high, opaque side walls afford this urban chapel a degree of privacy from public view, yet the high windows fill this sacred space with natural illumination. As daylight floods into the space from the continuous perimeter of clear glass clerestory windows, it is modulated by white metal exterior fins into a constantly changing pattern of light and shadow.

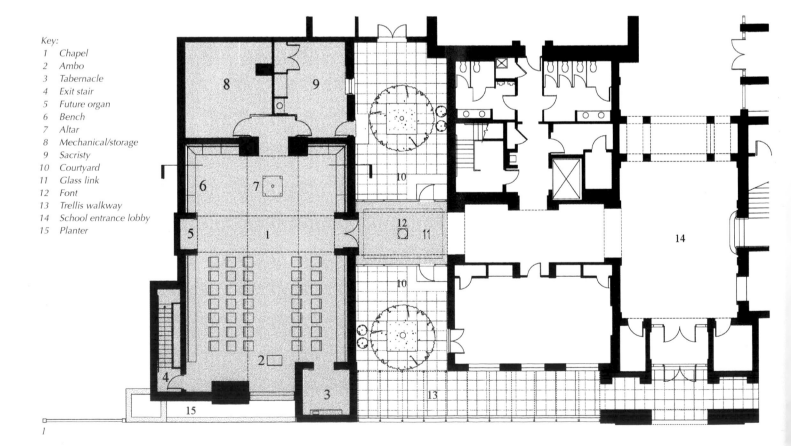

Key:
1   Chapel
2   Ambo
3   Tabernacle
4   Exit stair
5   Future organ
6   Bench
7   Altar
8   Mechanical/storage
9   Sacristy
10 Courtyard
11 Glass link
12 Font
13 Trellis walkway
14 School entrance lobby
15 Planter

1

2

4

6

3

5

7

1   Floor plan
2   The chapel establishes a presence in its urban
    setting
3   The chapel interior is spacious and light
4   Brick walls along the sidewalk afford the
    chapel privacy
5   High windows allow light but limit views inside
6   The tabernacle tower is a landmark on the
    streetscape
7   Lantern of tower captures light and modulates it
Photography: Kenneth M. Wyner

TEMPLE BETH SHALOM

Hastings-on-Hudson, New York, USA

Perkins Eastman Architects PC, in association with Edward I. Mills & Associates, designed this new synagogue and religious school for a 400-family synagogue. The facility was built on a steep wooded three-acre site overlooking the Hudson River and next to the old Croton aqueduct. The new two-story synagogue building, which encompasses 15,000 square feet, is carefully designed into the hillside so that it appears to be growing from it.

A central circulation spine running perpendicular to the site slope organizes the various program elements. At the lower level the entry lobby and formal stair divide the synagogue's administrative offices from the classroom wing. The stair, which is an elegant assemblage of rectilinear and curved forms, leads to the upper level. Here the circulation spine separates the sanctuary, library, and chapel from the function hall. As one processes from the ground-level entrance to the sanctuary, space grows in height as well as importance. Throughout, the spaces are marked with a liberal use of natural light.

The concept incorporates a variety of movable walls which allow spaces to open up to each other. This flexibility was important in order to accommodate a variety of functions and audience sizes. The sanctuary can be expanded to occupy nearly the entire level, as walls can be moved in the classroom areas. A small chapel to the east of the main sanctuary can also be incorporated into the large space for important holy days. In addition, clerestory lighting and large expanses of windows in the main sanctuary visually open the space to the building's naturally wooded site, and delivers light deep into the building.

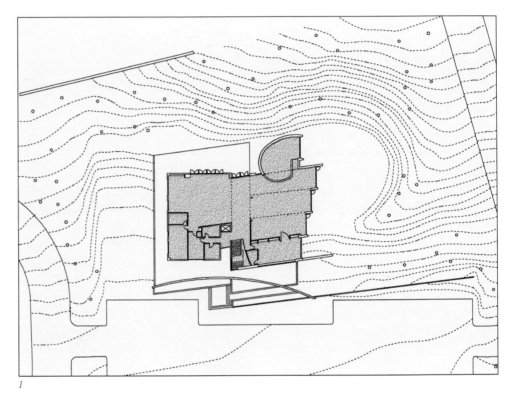

1

2

1 Site plan
2 The library is an important space for study in the synagogue
3 As it faces south, the building steps back with glazed walls to admit light
4 The synagogue's entry facade splays back in a welcoming gesture
5 The entrance to the building is modulated and accented with landscape elements
6 Thin layer peels off the facade to extend the splayed elevation
7 View through the sanctuary toward the chapel
8 View from the second floor over the staircase with its natural illumination
9 Lobby is distinguished by a free-standing stair bathed in natural light
10 View from the chapel through the sanctuary
11 The sanctuary space is filled with sunlight and angles

Photography: Chuck Choi

REORGANIZED CHURCH OF JESUS CHRIST OF LATTER DAY SAINTS TEMPLE

Independence, Missouri, USA

L eaders of the Reorganized Church of Jesus Christ of Latter Day Saints (RLDS) envisioned their temple and world headquarters as distinguished from all other religious structures. It was to be an architectural expression of growth, dynamism, unity, and international presence. The design by Hellmuth, Obata + Kassabaum (HOK) is inspired by the intricate spiral of the chambered nautilus seashell, a form governed by the same natural laws that shaped the human umbilical cord, rams' horns, and nebulas found in space. Symbolizing nature, found all over the world and in many different cultures, the spiral appears to be a fitting symbol of RLDS's worldwide presence. The basic form of the temple was studied using a simple computer program which generated the three-dimensional surface of the form. Computer imaging and large-scale interior models were used to refine the sanctuary space for optimum acoustics and sight lines. The three-dimensional complexity of all the major architectural components, including the

Continued

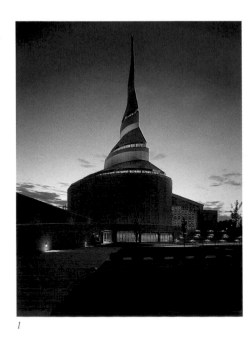

1 The temple's spire is a complex spiral shape
2 The curving Worshiper's Path has textured concrete walls
3 Exit foyer is illuminated through a colorful stained glass window

3

4

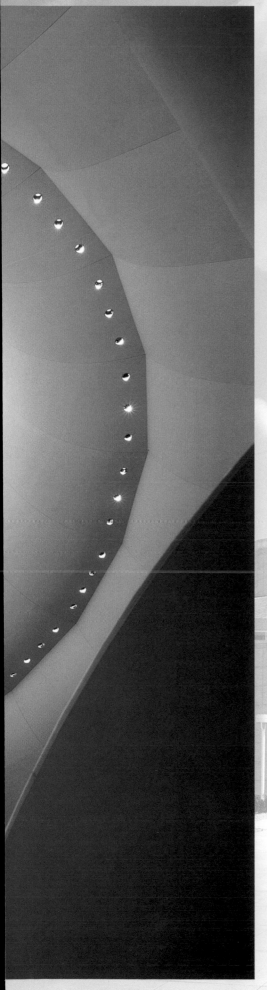

5

6

4   *The spiral in the sanctuary billows like a cloud above*
5   *The focus of the sanctuary is a large pipe organ*
6   *Entry lobby to the temple and administration complex*
7   *Floor plan*

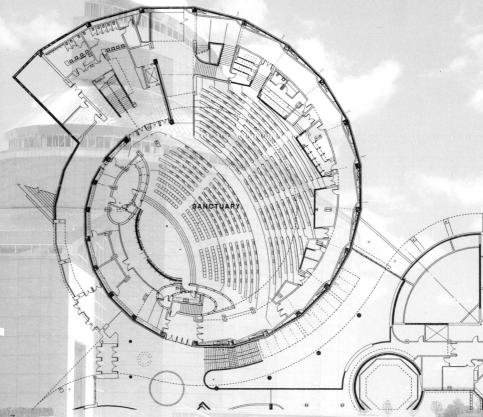

7

compound curves of the warping, spiraling ceiling, were designed, developed, and defined in space relative to the controlling 3-D form model. The temple sanctuary seats more than 1,800 people in a circular arrangement creating a sense of intimacy. From its base, the temple whirls upward, tapering to form a spire that peaks at 300 feet. As a logarithmic shape, the temple's curves become broader in a geometric progression in each revolution of the spiral, providing an upwardly focusing image uniquely suitable for a place of worship. The exterior is clad in granite with a strip of clerestory glass that follows the spiral form, bathing the temple's interior with light. A school and offices are housed in an L-shaped wing that wraps around the southern edge of the temple. A two-story reception hall, which is topped by a skylight, is located in the transitional space between the sanctuary and the school and office wing.

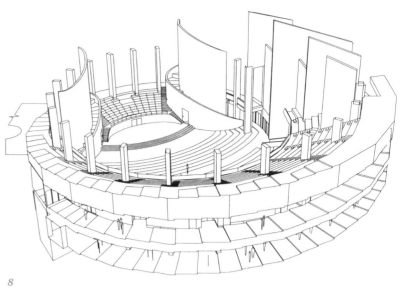

8

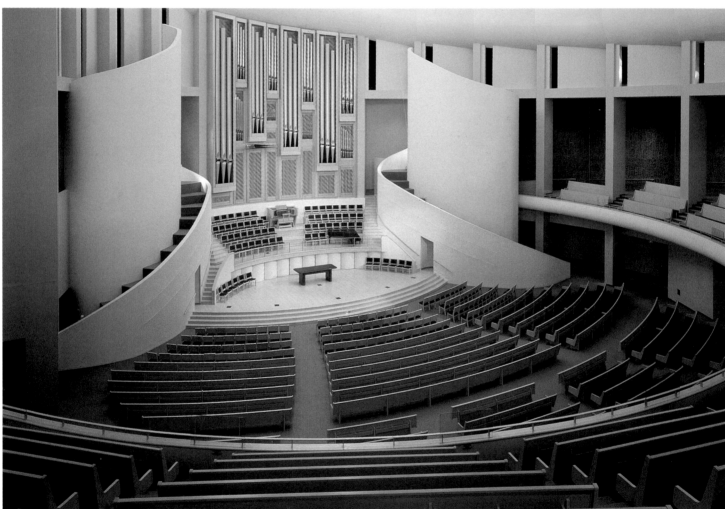

9

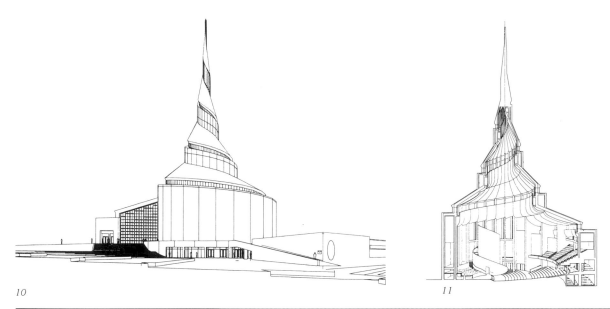

10

11

12

8   *Computer study, sanctuary chamber*
9   *View of the altar, choir area, and organ from the sanctuary back*
10   *View to northeast*
11   *Section looking northwest*
12   *Conference room in the temple complex is intimately scaled*
Photography: Balthazar Korab

IMMACULATE CONCEPTION CHURCH

St. Mary's County, Maryland, USA

This new church, with seating for 420, replaces a facility that became too small to serve this growing parish. The architecture of the building, designed by Walton Madden Cooper Robinson Poness, complies with the wishes of the parish for a simple 'country church' to provide a link to the past and reflect the rural character of this southern Maryland community. The facade of the new building incorporates stained glass windows from the old church as a further means of recalling the original structure.

Liturgically, the building design follows the tenets of the Roman Catholic Church since Vatican II, which are further articulated in *Environment and Art in Catholic Worship* published by the National Conference of Catholic Bishops.

Parishioners enter the church through the bell tower that defines the narthex, found just before entering the nave. The nave is a simple space that unifies the congregation and the celebrants. As the Bishops' publication states, the liturgical space should have a good feeling in terms of human scale, hospitality, and graciousness, and this sanctuary captures the spirit of that description.

The sanctuary is raised on three steps with the altar centrally positioned for visibility and to denote its central role in the celebration of Mass. The tabernacle is set on a raised platform which terminates the processional axis that begins at the narthex.

Other key liturgical elements, the *ambo* (lectern for the reading of the gospel and sermons) and the baptismal font are placed in close proximity to the altar, fully visible by the congregation. The location of the choir and the musicians to the immediate side of the sanctuary allows visibility by the congregation. This placement enables the musicians to lead the musical liturgies as part of the congregation rather than as performers.

Exterior materials are white painted board and batten siding, masonry base, and asphalt shingle roofing. Interior materials include carpet, painted gypsum board, and painted steel trusses in the nave with textured, grooved plywood ceilings finished with a white semi-solid stain.

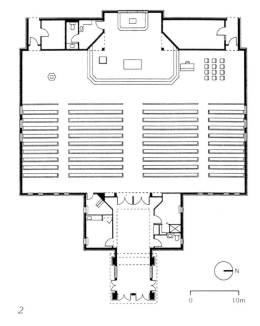

2

1

1 Elevation
2 Floor plan
3 Church exterior suggests the tradition of
  a country parish.

3

4

4 *Altar niche is small to promote a sense*
   of closeness
Opposite:
   Sanctuary interior is wide to promote a sense
   of intimate community
Photography: Kenneth M. Wyner

METROPOLITAN COMMUNITY CHURCH

Washington, DC, USA

The first American church built by a gay congregation (with a 25-year ministry) presented a unique challenge. It was understood that the building would have historical, social, and political significance as well as the opportunity to serve this congregation religiously.

The congregation and its architect, Suzane Reatig, wanted the design to relate to the mid-city context of row houses and low apartments, and yet to be immediately recognized as a church. It emerged as 'two buildings' (actually, two parts of the same structure); an L-shaped two-story masonry building for services, kitchen, bathrooms, administration offices, library, and chapel; and a sanctuary embraced by the masonry building on the east and north end and 'open' on the west and south.

The building's north face along Ridge Street is a two-story masonry facade in keeping with the row houses that line the block. As it turns the corner onto Fifth Street, the masonry wall begins to peel away revealing the building's core—a large barrel-vaulted structure of steel and glass

that radiates an openness towards the world outside and society. The church has a modest palette of materials; the walls are of gray-purple concrete block, the white-washed ceiling is corrugated metal, the steel frame construction is painted white, and glass encloses the frame.

The sanctuary glass—framed in aluminum and tinted a light gray-blue—lends a mirror-like effect reflecting the interior as well as the exterior. During daylight hours, some of the surroundings are mirrored in the glass, while at night the building glows with a calm inner light. Those inside the sanctuary see the tall trees outdoors, the sky, and birds soaring by. Because of the reflective coating of the glass, the building's interior is multiplied and a feeling of total blending of interior and exterior prevails.

While some urban churches choose to be fortresses from the city, this one with its glass refuses to shut out the city or to be shut out from it.

2

1

1 Block walls at corner afford some privacy
2 At night, the church hints at its interior
3 Site plan
4 Sanctuary is entered from south courtyard
Following pages:
  Reflective glass extends the perceived space

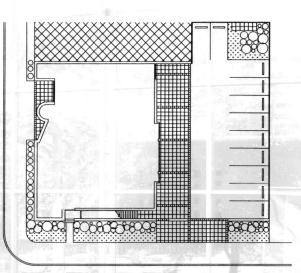

RIDGE STREET N.W.

FIFTH STREET N.W.

3

4

6 Floor plan
7 Sanctuary doors open to the south
Opposite:
    Sanctuary space has unbounded space and light
Photography: Robert Lautman

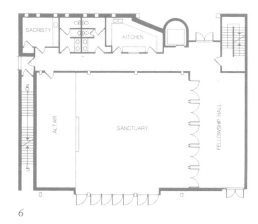

6

7

St. James Cathedral

Seattle, Washington, USA

1

St. James Cathedral was completed in 1907, and in 1916 the original dome over the crossing collapsed during a snow storm. The resulting repairs to the church dropped a vaulted ceiling over the crossing to hide the repair work. In 1994 work commenced on an US$8 million renovation and restoration of the historic church by The Bumgardner Architects with Fr. Richard Vosko as liturgical consultant, to accommodate the changing Roman catholic liturgy. This included locating the altar at the crossing, at the virtual center of the cathedral. Another goal of the renovation was to allow the cathedral's great volume to work with light. Reclaiming natural light was achieved through the insertion of a large oculus Dei (eye of God) at the crossing. The 14-foot diameter oculus is much smaller than the original dome, and it sits on a deep drum. This allows the introduction of natural light without direct sunlight for most of the year. The glazing in the oculus is clear so that the sky

and clouds can easily be seen. St. James has a sophisticated new lighting system throughout the cathedral that allows great diversity during the liturgical year. New chandeliers throughout the cathedral have up-lights for ambient lighting and down-lights for direct lighting. The lighting system allows 32 separate zones for the fixtures. Various combinations are possible, and one can preset the system for different liturgical events. Groups of lights can highlight architectural features or different locations around the cathedral, depending on the event. In contrast to this illuminated interior, the Marian Shrine northwest of the main altar is in total darkness, except for the glow of candlelight. Designed by local architect Susan Jones, the shrine recalls a cave, with a sensuously curved railing that traces the outline of a womb on the inside of the space. On the ceiling is a constellation of stars that replicates their position in the heavens on the day the cathedral was dedicated.

1   *Section through cathedral nave of new design*
2   *New glass in side altar affords privacy*
3   *View from the front entry up the central nave*
4   *The church unfolds from the new choir area*
Photography: James F. Housel

3

2

4

YOUNG ISRAEL OF BROOKLINE SYNAGOGUE

Brookline, Massachusetts, USA

After fire completely destroyed its 30-year-old temple, the Young Israel Orthodox congregation immediately began the task of rebuilding. Young Israel's goal was to rebuild on the same site while increasing the facility by 25 percent.

The program called for a beit nesset (main sanctuary) seating over 500 people, a beit midrash (chapel) to provide for daily services and to serve as a study hall and library, a social hall, and support facilities including administrative offices and three classrooms. The building, designed by Graham Gund Architects, is actively used throughout the day, beginning with morning prayer in the chapel and ending with evening study sessions in the classrooms.

Driving the building's siting and layout was the Halacha (Jewish law) which required the eastern orientation of both the sanctuary and the chapel so members pray facing Jerusalem. This presented a particular challenge due to site setback constraints and the need to angle these pieces off the prevailing street grid.

A second, albeit equally important, Halacha issue required the separation of men and women in the sanctuary. The design locates the majority of women's seating in a low balcony or gallery. The rest of the seating is on a raised platform on the ground floor, with sculpted ceilings. This is separated from the men's section by a unique mechitzah constructed of mill-work elements and sand-blasted Hebrew letters carved out of acrylic panels, with text from the first three verses of 'Eishet Chayil.' All of the women's seating in the main sanctuary, including the farthest seat in the upper corners of the balcony, is closer to the ark than any of the seats in the women's section were in the old shul.

The chapel of approximately 800 square feet, with its aron kodesh and book-lined walls and cabinets, provides a place of integration: prayer and learning come together as small groups of congregants gather for prayer at sunrise and sunset daily, with shiurim and study groups taking place here throughout the day and evening.

The design of the synagogue evolved around a theme of timeless imagery, tradition, and holiness. The new Young Israel Synagogue reinforces the congregation's own identity while placing it within the specific New England community.

1

2

3

4

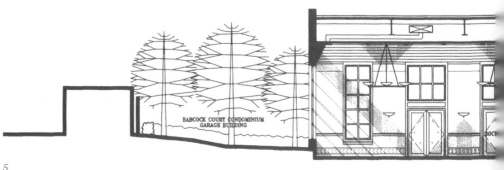

5

BABCOCK COURT CONDOMINIUM
GARAGE BUILDING

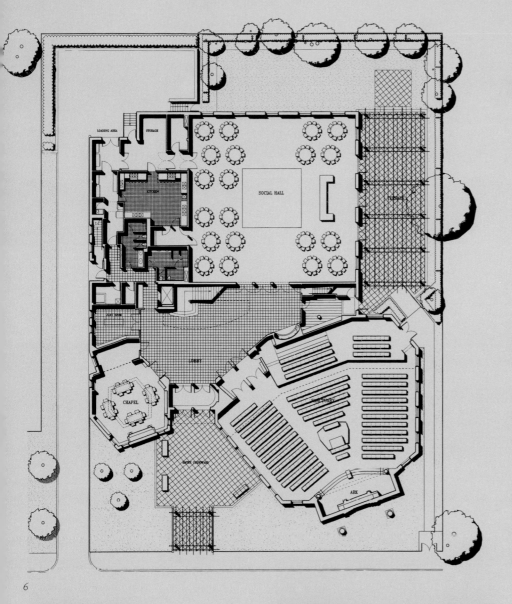

6

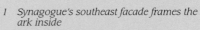

1 Synagogue's southeast facade frames the ark inside
2 View of sanctuary from the balcony
3 Sanctuary with the ark open
4 Ark enclosure replicates design on the southeast facade
5 Section
6 Site plan
7 Platform seating at the back of the sanctuary
8 Natural light permeates the interior
9 The lobby's ceremonial staircase
Photography: Steve Rosenthal

9

7

8

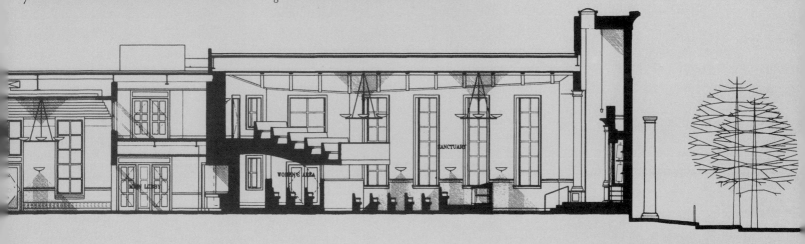

LIGHT OF THE WORLD CATHOLIC CHURCH

Littleton, Colorado, USA

Hoover Berg Desmond Architects (now AR7) was commissioned to design an 800-seat worship space and related support facilities for this young parish in a new suburban subdivision. The parish sought an architecture exemplifying basic, early Christian values, but at the same time an architecture natural to our time and culture.

An enclosed colonnade faces south and provides open-ended circulation to the east and west. Worship space, foyer, chapel, sacristy, cloister, and social hall adjoin the colonnade and are set into the hilltop to the north. Traditional early Christian forms—basilica, colonnade, cloister, and tower—are built of modest, contemporary materials such as brick, drywall, glue-laminated timber, composition shingles, and glass block. The steeple of the tower, with its mirror stainless steel and reflective glass, proclaims the 'Light of the World' to the neighborhood, day and night.

This building celebrates opposites and expresses their reconciliation. Throughout the building one finds the opposites of brick and glass, light and dark, indoors and outdoors, horizontal and vertical, circle and square, earth and wind, fire and water, as well as forms which can be seen as masculine and feminine, traditional and contemporary, sacred and secular. This attempt to celebrate and reconcile opposites is nowhere more evident than at the tower, the baptismal font, and the courtyard cross.

Continued

1   Main approach to entry
2   Courtyard cross is discreetly illuminated

1

2

3 Floor plan
4 The church in its landscape
5 Gallery extends across the church's facade

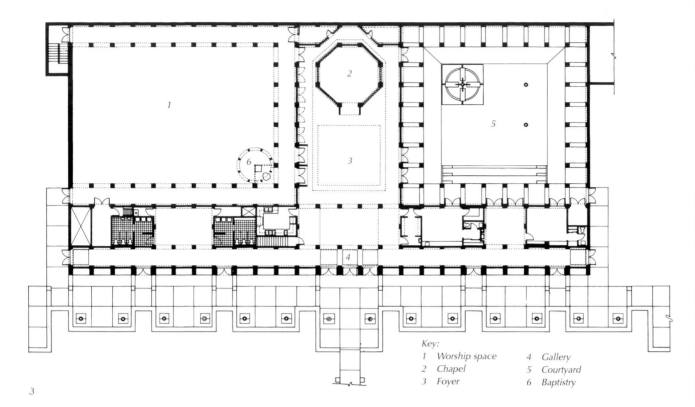

Key:
1 Worship space   4 Gallery
2 Chapel   5 Courtyard
3 Foyer   6 Baptistry

3

4   5

Opposite:
   Baptismal font is a dramatic focus
7 Baptismal font is within the sanctuary

7

The tower at the entrance provides a vertical element to balance the horizontality of the gallery. At the tower the simple forms of circle and square come together. Here the play of light and dark, the transition from brick to glass, and the capping of circle and square in a pyramid form is expressed. Baptism is the entry point of the Catholic Church and the baptismal font sits at the centerpoint of the tower. The font and the tower stand at the point of entry into the worship space. The circle of columns surrounding the font provides the threshold moment through which all pass to renew their own baptism before celebrating the Eucharist. In the same way that the tower and font speak of threshold and entrance, the courtyard cross speaks of journey and passage. The cross sculpture expresses the opposites of horizontal and vertical, polished and weathered surfaces, circle and square.

8

8 *Altar table is elegantly detailed*
9 *Altar furniture captures spirit of spare design*
Photography: R. Greg Hursley

9

CHAPEL OF THE WORD
AT DIVINE WORD MISSIONARIES

Techny, Illinois, USA

Divine Word Missionaries is a Roman Catholic religious order that carries out global missionary work in more than 60 countries. At the heart of Divine Word's Techny, Illinois headquarters lies Chapel of the Word. The complex housing Chapel of the Word consists of three existing adjoining buildings on a busy suburban road, in a large all-male religious community. Built over the past 100 years, the structures are radically different in style.

About 30 years ago, the exterior was wrapped in a 'kitschy' pseudo-Japanese facade. The buildings came together in an awkward way, with none of the various floor or ceiling elevations aligning. David Woodhouse Architects renovated and added a few thousand square feet to the first floor of the building to make the visitor center (a group of galleries whose exhibits showcase the order's missionary efforts around the world), a conference room and lounge (used for meeting and fund raising by the administrative staff upstairs), a religious gift store, and Chapel of the Word. The chapel is the destination for those who come to the visitor center, and is approached by a passage with plywood-lined surfaces tapering towards the chapel entry and a large, two-leaf pivot door. Alternately, the chapel

can be joined to the lounge space by opening hinged wood panels that are connected by steel rods to function as room-size double louvers. Chapel materials are bare and natural: birch veneer plywood; pine and cherry boards; galvanized sheet metal; slate; coir; and hand-sanded translucent plastic. The architect's design work is insertion, screening or cladding, clearly differentiated from what had been there before.

Formal references recall traditional Christian ecclesiastical architecture—the equation of light with the Divine presence; the steel pylons supporting the translucent fiberglass screens outside suggest buttresses; the chapel door is big and heavy with a little-man door contained in it like those in Gothic cathedrals; the axial organization of the chapel; the swirling, ascending clouds (with a couple of cherubim, too) make the ceiling reminiscent of a Roman Baroque church.

Mission Director Father Thomas Krosnicki describes the chapel as one in which 'Light—God's grace—pierces the boards, dispelling the inner darkness. A place of prayer where the Word is allowed to speak, to be heard, and received.'

2

1

3

1 The chapel's luminous skin glows at night
2 Slotted nature of the chapel wall allows visitors to leave prayers
3 Entry to the chapel is defined by a canopy
4 Chapel interior's light is diffuse and ethereal
5 Plywood walls part to allow entry to chapel
6 Chapel space is defined by stacked plywood walls
7 Interior wall surfaces are smooth and elegant
8 Approach to the chapel from plywood-lined passage
9 A juxtaposition of materials and finishes enlivens the chapel

Photography: Barbara Karant

4

6

8

5

7

9

ST. THOMAS MORE CATHOLIC CHURCH

Paducah, Kentucky, USA

St. Thomas More is a 25,000-square-foot church on a gently rolling 21-acre rural site in western Kentucky. Designed by Williamson Pounders Architects with Fr. Richard Vosko as liturgical consultant, the church's massing reflects the asymmetrical compositions of simple forms seen in the rural vernacular architecture of the region.

The buildings are clustered around an open plaza at the high point of the site in order to maximize views and catch summer breezes, and to make a strong statement to the community. The buildings are linked by a covered ambulatory recalling the monasteries of Europe. The plaza opens to the south to collect the warmth of the sun, and is enclosed on the other sides to afford protection from winter winds. A bell tower marks the church as one approaches from a distance.

The building is a metaphor for the people of God who are the members of the church. Thus, it serves as a resonator of their traditions and their visions. The walkways remind them that they are pilgrims. The central plaza embraces them. The doors represent a sheep gate, like the Christ of the gospels.

Continued

1   The church is sited on a gentle hill, overlooking a pond
2   Site plan
3   The church opens to a cloister where visitors enter
4   Detail of sanctuary space, distinguished with its elegant brackets

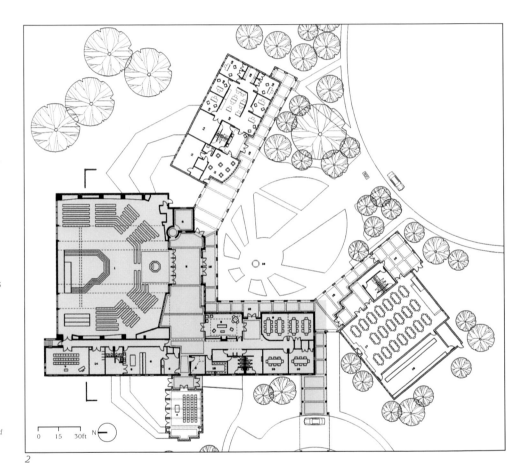

2

0   15   30ft   N

1

3

4

Outdoor liturgical gatherings take place in the
central plaza, while a large interior gathering
space offers hospitality to all members and
visitors. Clear glass doors welcome the
worshipers into the nave where a baptismal font
with flowing water is placed near the entry. The
font is a multi-valent life-giving symbol, a place
for both baptism and burial.

A noble but simple setting for the liturgical
celebration is created in the nave through the use
of natural materials and light. The architects also
designed all liturgical furniture. The main
worship space overlooks a pond to the north
through a wall of windows. Natural light also
enters the large volume through oversized
clerestories.

The semi-circular seating pattern creates a sense
of unity and fosters active participation during
the liturgy. The natural acoustics foster a joyful
song. The tower chapel, where the Eucharist is
reserved, is a place for private prayer as well as a
beacon to the world.

5

6

ISLAMIC CULTURAL CENTER

New York, New York, USA

The Islamic Cultural Center is the first mosque and religious center for New York City's Muslim community. The design by Skidmore, Owings & Merrill is intended to formulate an architectural expression that represents the rich and varied traditions of the Muslim world in the context of the 20th century. The Center is located on a 200-foot by 240-foot site, bounded by Third Avenue and 96th and 97th Streets. The original master plan consists of a 1,000-person mosque, a minaret (designed by another architect), an adjoining administrative building that will contain classrooms for teaching the Koran, a library, and administrative offices. The mosque is oriented toward Mecca as required by religious law. As such, its placement on the site is rotated and skewed off the city grid. The positioning of the mosque creates a large open space that acts as a forecourt where worshipers can gather prior to the call for prayers, as is the tradition.

The prayer hall is entered through a monumental portal fronting the court. The upper portion of the portal is formed by a composition of squares and cubic inscriptions in carved relief. The lower portion consists of a pair of 15-foot-high bronze doors. In the opened position, as they would be during the ceremonies, layers of glass panels suspended from the structure above are revealed. Each layer of glass is cut in a series of steps to ultimately resemble an arch recalling traditional stalactite portals. Beyond the portal is a vestibule that acts as a transitional zone to the religious realm and as a weather barrier.

From inside the prayer hall, the view is unobstructed in every direction and to the full height of the perimeter walls. Natural light plays an important role in defining and enhancing the interior space. Light is filtered into the space through the large glazed areas set within the trusses and which are patterned with fired ceramic surface decoration reflecting an Islamic design. A circular mass of lights suspended by cords from the underside of the dome form a low roof of light above the congregation.

1

1 Exterior is a combination of traditional and
   contemporary forms
2 Elevation
3 Building form expresses the large, cubic
   sanctuary within

4   Portal is framed with contemporary versions
    of Islamic decorative art
5   Dome above the sanctuary expresses an elegant
    and simple design
Opposite:
    The sanctuary is filled with light delivered from
    clerestories and reveals around wall panels
Photography: Wolfgang Hoyt

4

5

GETHSEMANE EPISCOPAL CATHEDRAL

Fargo, North Dakota, USA

This new cathedral, designed by Moore/ Andersson Architects, replaces a nearby historic structure destroyed by fire. Rather than rebuild on its in-town, infill site, the congregation opted to move just outside of the center onto a clear site that offers room for expansion.

The cathedral is organized by a cruciform plan. Entry is through the cross axis linking an intimate 40-seat chapel and the narthex with a courtyard and covered loggia access to support spaces. The worship space accommodates 350 people with expansion to double that capacity in the great hall to the west of the sanctuary. All of the furniture and elements in the sanctuary are movable to allow flexibility in responding to future worship needs. Classrooms and support spaces, including offices for the bishop and diocese offices, are grouped to the north of the entry and sanctuary to create a buffer to protect the larger volume of the cruciform from winter winds. This arrangement also reduces the perceived mass of the building from residences to the north.

The sculptural mass of the building to the south and southeast speaks to a traditional church image, while exterior materials of whitewashed board and batten siding, metal standing seam, and green shingle roofs relate to the vernacular farm buildings of the region. Interior materials are simple: concrete block walls, concrete floors, and painted wood trusses provide a subdued backdrop to brightly colored, light and sound diffusing ceiling panels. The woodwork recalls the ornament of the original church. As a special repository is found in the great hall, artifacts rescued from the fire are honored in a 'memory palace' to keep the image of the old cathedral alive, while the new cathedral carries this congregation into the next century.

1   *A commanding presence, the cathedral is made up of an assemblage of Gothic inspired elements*
2   *Section*
3   *Crisp detailing is celebrated with the rake of the sun, giving the cathedral texture*

1

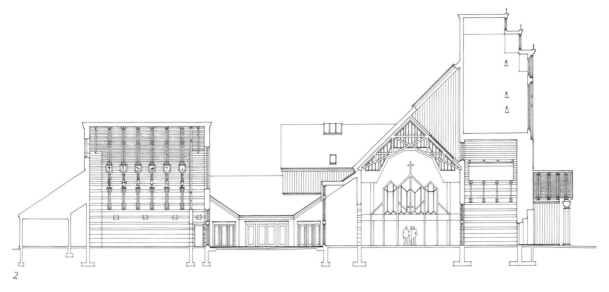

2

3

4 Floor plan
5 The austere chapel, with its colorful brackets, is an intimate setting for worship
6 The sanctuary space is a combination of color, light, and simple materials
Photography: Timothy Hursley

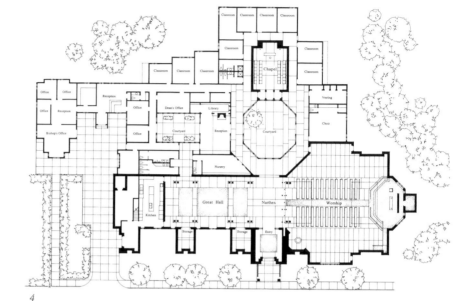

4

5

6

JOSEPH SLIFKA CENTER FOR JEWISH LIFE AT YALE

New Haven, Connecticut, USA

Located on an urban site on the Yale University campus, this building is designed by Roth and Moore Architects to serve the religious and cultural needs of the Jewish community of faculty, students, and staff. Earlier facilities were located in obscure basement corners of the campus.

A matrix of spaces was defined to bring together various constituencies within the academic community, including Orthodox, Conservative, and Reform branches of Judaism. The goal was to nurture spiritual character, an aspect of student life not always present in the intellectual climate of the 20th century university.

The building contains 20,000 square feet distributed on four floors. Facilities include a 275-seat dining hall with separate meat and dairy kitchens; living room for informal gatherings; a beit midrash (chapel) for daily religious services; a student activity center; Judaic library with adjacent study spaces; rabbi's study; staff offices; and multi-purpose room for religious services, lectures, concerts, movies, theater, art exhibits, and Israeli dancing.

An outdoor terrace surrounded by a garden wall encloses a permanent sukkah seating 60, a symbolic shelter for taking meals during the fall harvest festival of Succoth. An early premise was to create an open and inviting building while allowing disparate activities to occur simultaneously. The spatial organization has virtually no corridors where activities might appear hidden and seemingly private. On a Sabbath morning, three religious services are held at the same time: the Orthodox service in the beit midrash, the egalitarian Conservative service in the multi-purpose room, and the Reform service in the living room.

A poured-in-place concrete structural frame was chosen for its acoustic mass in addition to its potential for architectural expression. The 16" exterior masonry wall with 4" cavity provides an exceptionally well insulated environment. Interior wall surfaces throughout are unpainted ground face block. Floor materials are quarry tile, oak, or carpet. Ceilings are primarily exposed structure.

1

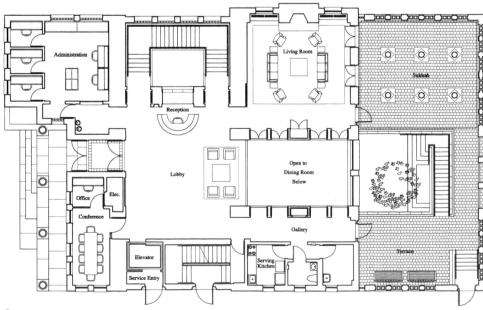

2

3

1   *The south side of the building is distinguished by generous overhangs for shade*
2   *Entry level floor plan*
3   *View of terrace through arched gateway toward sukkah*

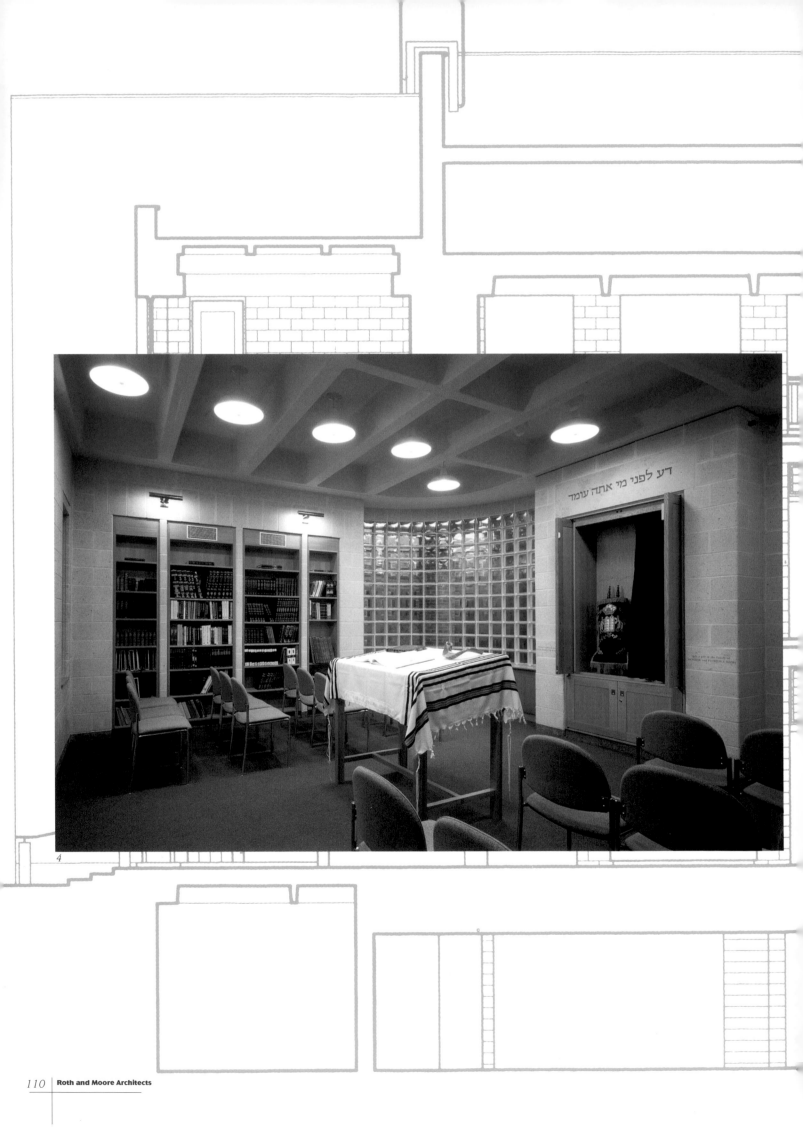

4

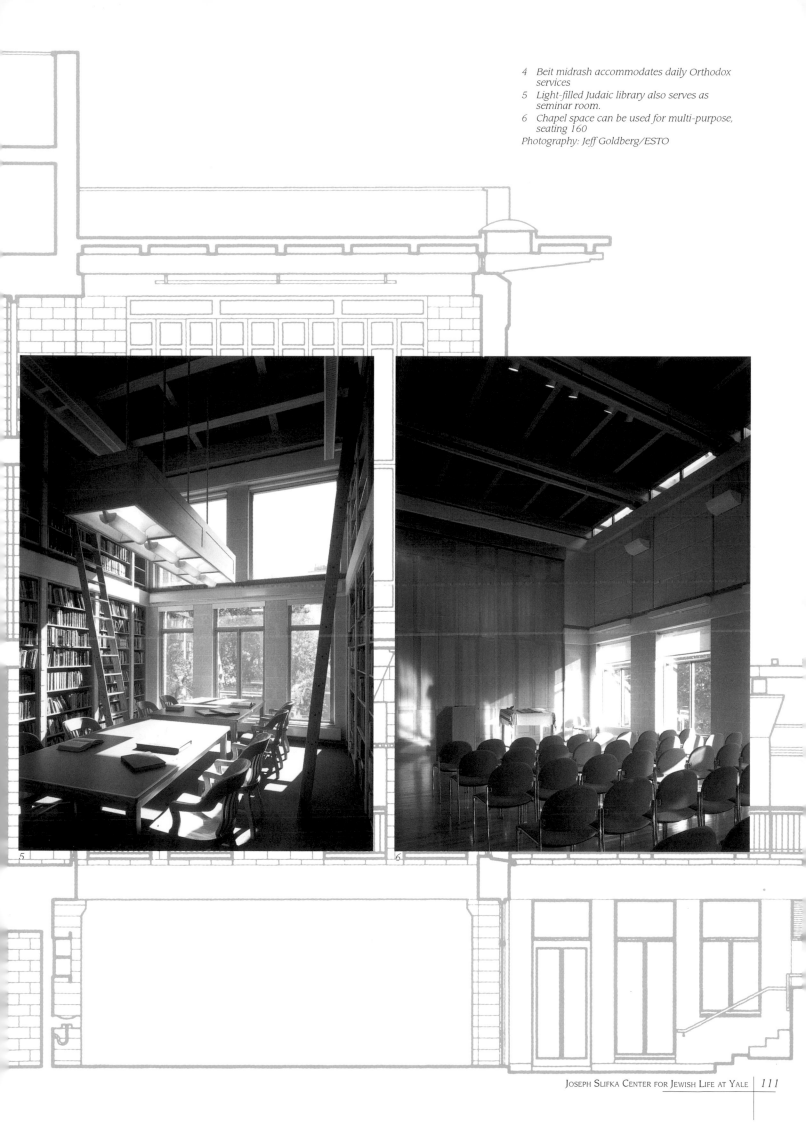

4 Beit midrash accommodates daily Orthodox services
5 Light-filled Judaic library also serves as seminar room.
6 Chapel space can be used for multi-purpose, seating 160
Photography: Jeff Goldberg/ESTO

5

6

MEPKIN ABBEY CHURCH

Moncks Corner, South Carolina, USA

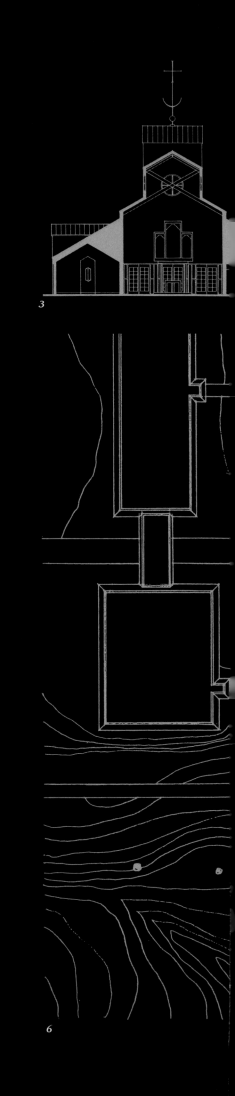

3

In 1949 a group of monks began monastic life at Mepkin, a famous 1700s rice plantation located along the Cooper River in South Carolina's 'low country.' The property belonged to Henry R. Luce and Clare Boothe Luce who donated it for the new monastery. Over the years, the community developed a style of liturgy and monastic hospitality whereby their pre-Vatican II space no longer suited their needs. The new church, designed by Hammel, Green and Abrahamson, Inc. expresses the identity of this monastic community and vision for the future.

The church is sited at the heart of the Abbey—a complex of stucco buildings or 'houses' including dormitories, refectory, chapter room, library, scriptorium, and guest-house. The church is not just another structure in this complex, but the first house among houses. The plan of the church has a central nave with several ancillary spaces around it for easy and private access. The building is developed on a three-meter module that grounds the sense of order and simplicity so dominant in monastic life. Because the Abbey is cloistered, there is a separate entrance porch for guests and retreatants and two entrance porches for the monks.

In this project, the centrality of the altar to the space, the relationship of the monastic choir to the altar, the relationship of retreatants to the monks, and the placement of the guests or casual visitors speak to the theology life. The design also includes a smaller, intimate space for private prayer. A separate bell tower not only calls the community to worship, but plays a significant role in the liturgy of services.

Construction methods and materials were used that were indigenous to the area. Because the church is in a sub-tropical region, natural air movement is encouraged through large screen doors at the porches and the clerestory windows, allowing ventilation during warm times of the year. Windows are carefully placed to bring daylight and luminosity to the space.

1 *Exterior creates a memorable profile*
2 *The church and its tower dominate monastic life*
3 *Section*
4 *Altar table occupies the central crossing*
5 *The elegant but simple sanctuary is appropriately monastic*
6 *Site plan*
Photography: courtesy HGA

1

2

6

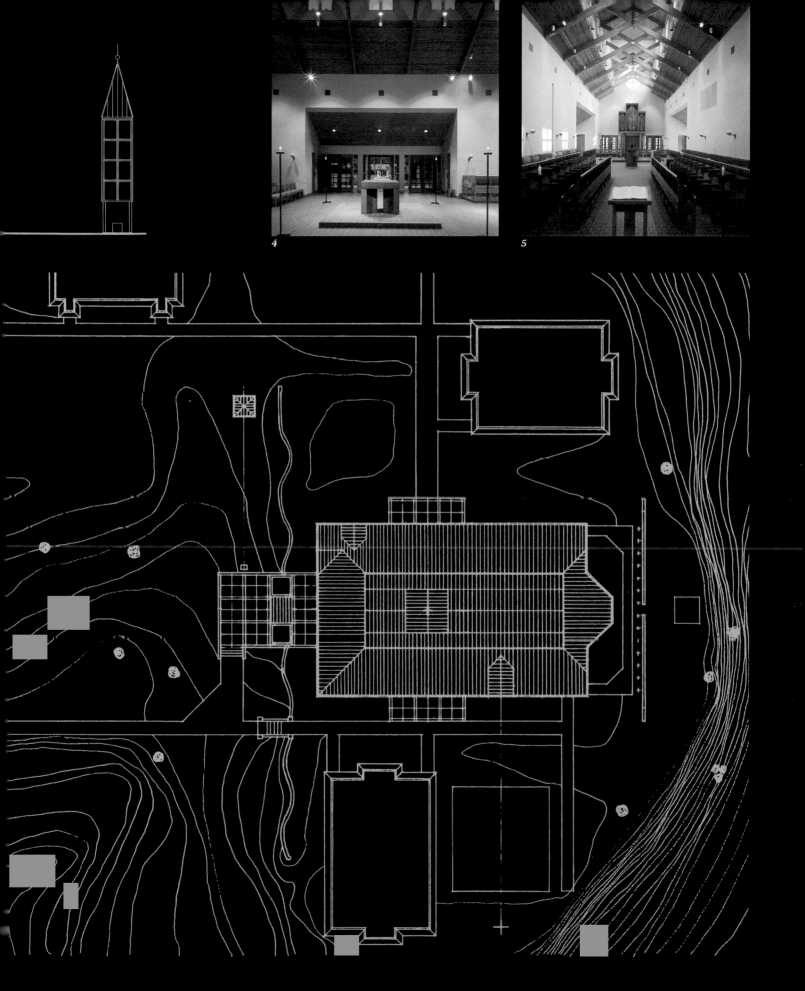

4

5

SEAMAN'S CHURCH INSTITUTE

New York, New York, USA

Designed by Polshek and Partners Architects, this building houses a 160-year-old, non-profit, Episcopalian, benevolence organization for merchant seafarers. The design incorporates and preserves the facade of a four-story structure dating from 1799 and holds the existing street wall in Manhattan's South Street Seaport Historic District.

The primary and public program element is the ecumenical chapel, located opposite the main entrance on the ground floor. The chapel skylights effect a conceptual separation from the rest of the building, reinforcing the idea of a safe haven. Likewise the sand-blasted glass door separates the energy of the street from the serenity of the chapel while its translucency draws the visitor inward.

Its proportions and materials allow the chapel to function equally well as a locus for silent and individual contemplation, religious services and non-religious activities. The chapel is accessible to the public and is used as much by the immediate community as by merchant seafarers.

While overt religious symbolism is limited to the cross and liturgical blue and gold, reinforcing the nondenominational character of the space, nautical imagery abounds. The lofty proportions of the narrow, double-height space and the chapel's curved ceiling are analogous to the proportions and forms of the hull of a ship. In the manner of traditional seafarer's chapels, a votive ship model (offered by the captain of the ship to ensure safe passage to the home port), is suspended from the ceiling at the front wall. The 150-year-old baptismal font takes the form of a capstan, and a ship's figurehead surmounts the door. The blue sand-blasted clerestory window depicts a map of the heavens, a reference to those legendary sailors for whom the stars provided their only reliable guide.

1   The Institute overlooks the city's waterfront, and suggests a nautical spirit in its architecture
2   Exploded floor plan

1

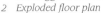

2

3   *High above the chapel, the ceiling rolls in*
     a curve that suggests a sail
4   *The chapel space is intimate and private with*
     subtle color, to encourage quiet contemplation
5   *Ground floor lobby is dominated by a staircase*
     that seems to float through the ceiling
Photography: Jeff Goldberg/Esto Photographics

3

4

5

CHRIST CONGREGATIONAL CHURCH

Brockton, Massachusetts, USA

Designed by Donham & Sweeney, this 450-member Congregational Church enjoys a religious history dating back to the 1700s. Merged from four separate parishes in the 1980s and housed in an older church that offered little room for expansion, the growing congregation decided to build a new church that would architecturally reflect its distinguished past and spiritually create a stronger sense of unity.

Congregationalism has its antecedent in the Puritan movement, which called for the return to pure roots in worship. It also extolled simplification and a stripping away of ornament and other architectural and decorative excess. The Puritans' meeting house was a simple building. It expressed the simple, unambiguous, and rigorous nature of their civic and religious life. The sanctuary allowed the congregation to

have close contact with the speaker. The service was a liturgy of the Word. The spoken Word from the Bible and the sermonizing on the Word were prime. There was no need to accommodate processions or other movements.

The new Christ Church building clearly grows out of this tradition of church design. It is honest, straightforward, filled with light, and (like the congregation it serves) 'worship-centered.' Worship is a collective activity, so the design focuses on the 450-seat sanctuary where there is a strong sense of togetherness. A square room, symmetrical on all sides, has the best sense of 'oneness.' Turning the room 45 degrees gives it a distinctive quality and allows for an open integration of the supporting spaces—the chapel, the chancel, and the organ/choir space.

Inside the sanctuary, the unobstructed clear span creates an expressive structural form that soars to the light in the cupola. An Austin pipe organ and the altar's custom-designed cross are central focal points of the space. Seating and pews can be rearranged to provide for flexibility of use.

A generous and distinctive narthex, which includes two stained glass windows and a large painting from their former church, was designed in response to the congregation's tradition of greeting one another in Christian fellowship before the service. The narthex also provides an important link between the upper and lower level entrances, as well as the library and lower-lever fellowship hall, classrooms, kitchens, offices and support spaces.

1

1 South elevation contains walk-out entrance to lower-level fellowship hall
2 The church nestles into a hill, surrounded with mature landscaping
3 West elevation reveals the design's simple forms and symbols

2

3

Previous pages:
  Interior is open, light, and airy, with expressive
  roof structure
5 Traditional pews with simple detailing reinforce
  the refined interior
6 Site plan
7 Organ dominates the south wall of the
  sanctuary, which also includes choir seating
8 Floor plan
Photography: Steve Rosenthal

5

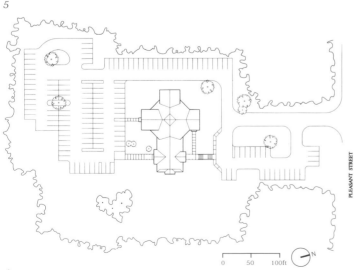

6

7

PLEASANT STREET

0   50   100ft   N

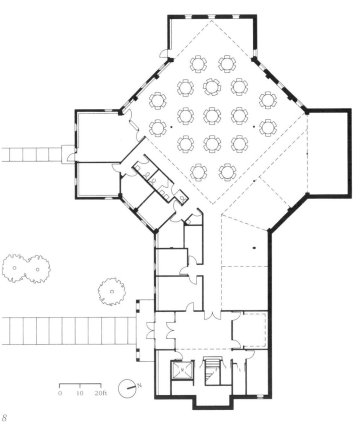

8

SAN JUAN BAUTISTA MISSION

Miami, Florida, USA

Built with a modest budget, the San Juan Bautista Mission, designed by Duany Plater-Zyberk & Company, was made possible by a coordinated effort and commitment of many parishioners, local professionals, and neighborhood residents who volunteered their time and resources. The mission building affords nearby parishioners the opportunity of walking to church or other social events without having to drive to the main parish complex. It functions primarily as a place of worship and provides endless possibilities for neighborhood interaction by hosting varied social activities, including those of other civic institutions. It also provides a location for children of the community to attend programs such as CCD. The mission thus functions as both a spiritual center and as a resource facility for the largely poor Latin American residents of the area. It also serves the community's specific needs by providing medical, legal, and financial counseling as well as immigration advice. The building's design

clearly alludes to the traditional neighborhood churches of Latin America and the Caribbean, offering a courtyard as a refuge from the hectic urban environment outside.

Located on a 50-foot by 104-foot lot, the building makes optimum use of its site with minimum side and rear setbacks and through the placement of a low front building at the sidewalk. This single-story wing houses an office and a small chapel, providing much-needed street definition by reinforcing the frontage line. The front facade is a simple wall with modest decoration framing the entrance opening. The zaguan is a shaded vestibule that connects the street to a sun-lit, cloistered courtyard containing an octagonal baptismal fountain and a bell tower. The inner nave of the small church is cruciform in shape with a central altar. Large clerestory windows flood the space with light and a figurative ceiling mural by a local artist provides the strongest ornamental feature.

1

2

1   From the street, the mission presents a simple,
    dignified presence.
2   The ceiling of the sanctuary is adorned with
    a vibrant fresco
3   View from the courtyard's center to the street
    entrance
4   Courtyard offers shade and quiet solace,
    in the middle of an urban neighborhood

3

4

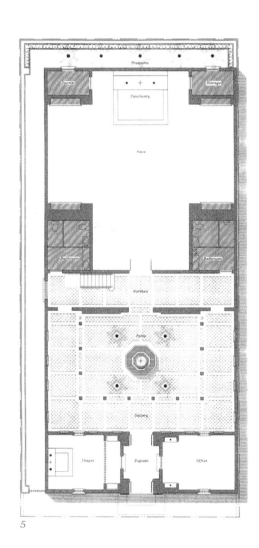

5

5 Ground floor plan
6 The mission presents an interior facade to
   the courtyard
Opposite:
   *Entry into the zaguan frames views of the
   courtyard*
Photography: Carlos Morales

6

ST. GREGORY'S EPISCOPAL CHURCH

San Francisco, California, USA

S t. Gregory's Episcopal Church, designed by Goldman Architects, reflects a unique, historically inspired liturgy based on 4th and 5th century Christian worship and its Jewish antecedents. In St. Gregory's worship services there are two distinct aspects: the Liturgy of the Word (Bible readings) and the Liturgy of Eucharist (Holy Communion). The church building form, a gabled structure joined to an octagonal structure, comes from the creation of two distinct but linked worship areas, each with their own liturgical and acoustical requirements —one for the Liturgy of the Word and one for the Liturgy of Eucharist.

The gabled structure, for the Liturgy of the Word, has a roof supported by exposed glulam and sawn lumber trusses. The room seats 200 people on two sides, facing each other across a central platform. The presider's chair is located at the north end of the platform, beneath the 60-foot-high belltower, in front of a pre-eminent focal point: a 20-foot-high painted icon depicting the mystical marriage of Christ with the believer's soul. Bible readings in this room take place from a lectern at the opposite, south end of the platform. The antiphonal seating encourages spoken and sung community participation and a sense of connection between all congregants.

Midway through the service, worshipers move in a procession from this worship area to the octagonal room for the Liturgy of Eucharist, spiraling into place around the wood altar table at the center of the room, below the 60-foot-high cupola. The centralizing form of this octagonal room is ideal for this kind of movement and liturgical activity.

Continued

1

1 Dormers and bell tower of this wooden building suggest Russian churches
2 East elevation of the church fronts the street and welcomes visitors
3 Floor plan
4 This entry is distinguished by a mosaic work by local artists

2

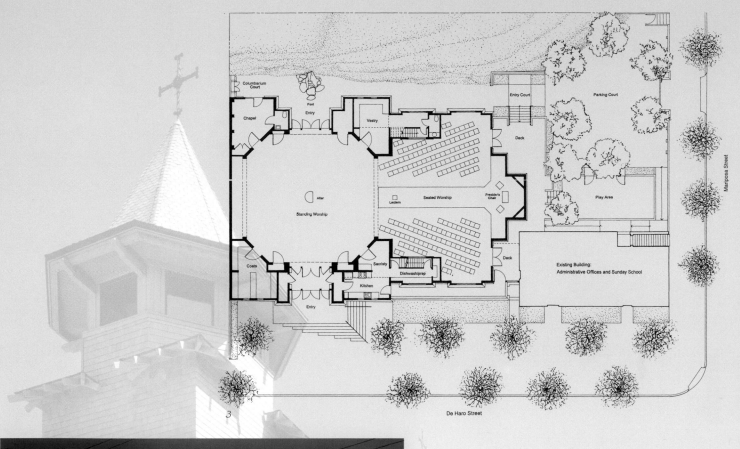

3

4

The church extends the San Francisco Bay
Region tradition of architecture with its intimate
connections between indoor and outdoor garden
courts, abundant daylight, and exuberantly
expressed wood structural elements. Along the
west of the St. Gregory's site is a steep, ivy-
covered serpentine rock hillside. A garden path
between the church and hill leads to a garden
court entry on the west side of the worship area
for the Liturgy of Eucharist. The baptismal font is
in this garden court beside the hill, on cross axis
with the altar table. Water springs from the top of
the rock font and flows down into a carved basin.

5

5   Section
6   An intricate wood structure crowns the standing
    worship area

6

7

8

7 View of the seated worship area, towards
   president's chair and icon by local artist
8 View from the standing worship area to the
   seated worship area

Photography: Charles Callister, Jr. (4);
Jane Lidz (1,2,6,7,8)

KOL HAVERIM SYNAGOGUE

Glastonbury, Connecticut, USA

Designed by Arbonies King Vlock Architects, this modest project renovates an existing building (a former Knights of Columbus hall) for classrooms and a library. This reborn older structure is enhanced with a new addition, devoted to offices, a social hall, and a new sanctuary.

The new synagogue is appropriately understated, using traditional materials, such as wood shingle siding. The parking lot is not visible from the road or foreground to the experience of arrival. To achieve this, the face of the sanctuary addition is turned nearly perpendicular to the street to create a sense of enclosure. A sweeping loggia extends the welcoming perception of the entrance closer to parking.

The continuous drape of the roof unifies the building form. The loggia creates layers of space and mediates between exterior and interior, dramatizing the experience of moving from the temporal to the spiritual. Once inside, the vertical space of the entrance lobby, soaring to the light above, creates a sense of uplift and expectation. The Star of David cut into the vertical wall plane above the sanctuary doors serves as a powerful icon of Judaism and a ceremonial gateway to the sanctuary beyond. Here, an historic ark dating from the 1800s is given a suitable new home. The gabled end embraces this sacred artifact, bathing it with diffuse natural light.

A major design issue common to all synagogues is how to reconcile the need for capacity and intimacy. On most occasions, the sanctuary must offer an intimate setting for 50 to 75 worshipers. However, life's most important events—the high holy days, weddings, Bar and Bat Mitzvahs—require large spaces. A concealed movable wall between the sanctuary and the social hall combined with the orientation of the ark allows the sanctuary space to be extended easily for larger ceremonies without sacrificing intimacy.

1

1 Entrance to the synagogue's new wing
   is protected by a welcoming portico
2 Illuminated, the synagogue interior offers views
   of colorful symbols inside

2

3–5   Symbols of Judaism adorn stained glass
       windows
  6   Sanctuary space is dominated by the 19th
       century ark preserved from the earlier
       synagogue
  7   Floor plan
  8   Multi-faceted ceiling gives the new sanctuary
       space a variegated quality
  9   Site plan
Following pages:
      Color and symbolism give the entrance lobby
      added interest
Photography: courtesy Arbonies King Vlock
Architects (3–5): Timothy Hursley (1,2,6,8)

3

4

5

6

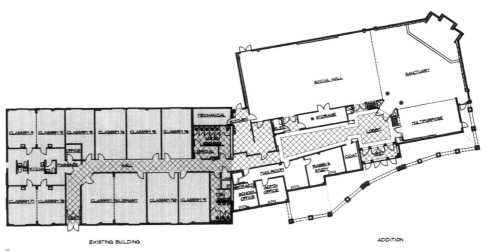

EXISTING BUILDING   ADDITION

7

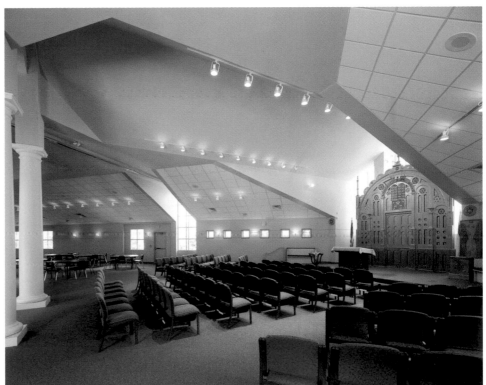

8

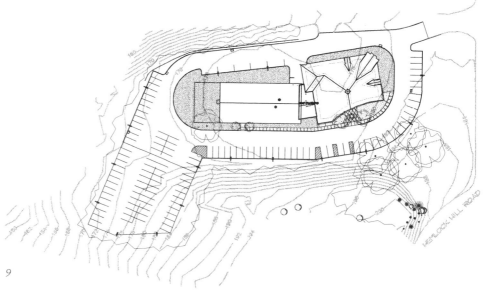

9

CENTENARY UNITED METHODIST CHURCH

Lexington, Kentucky, USA

Centenary Methodist congregation, established more than 40 years ago, saw the construction of a new church, designed by Omni Architects, as an opportunity to create an entirely new campus on a new site.

The church complex is placed on the 14-acre site to maximize the building area, yet with a minimum of disturbance of the existing site features and views. The church's placement at the high point of the site gives it added stature.

The program includes three major components: worship space, education space, and fellowship space. The final design is organized around a central courtyard that literally connects the narthex with the fellowship hall activities.

The fellowship hall is found at the north end of the complex, and includes ample recreation space. To the east is the education wing, with classroom and administration spaces. The sanctuary is found to the south, and is marked with natural light from above and crisp, simple detailing. The structure and organization of the building is rooted in the use of masonry as the prime building material.

The meditation garden is designed to provide a link between the sanctuary, educational, and recreational wings of the complex. It also serves as a setting for events such as arts and crafts' fairs, performances, and liturgical processions. The fountain design is derived from the biblical notion of the 'River of Life.' As the water flows from the sanctuary, it traverses gently through the space and spills into a quiet pool. A separate cloistered garden is found behind brick walls at the base of the bell tower. This space is designed for personal meditation with an atmosphere of quiet solitude.

1 Floor plan
2 Axonometric
3 *The altar area is dominated by a large organ and choir seating, with a rose window illuminated from above*
4 *The apse end of the church describes a gentle curve on the south wall*
5 *Seating is arranged in a wide distribution, allowing closer proximity to the altar*
Photography: Walt Roycraft Photography

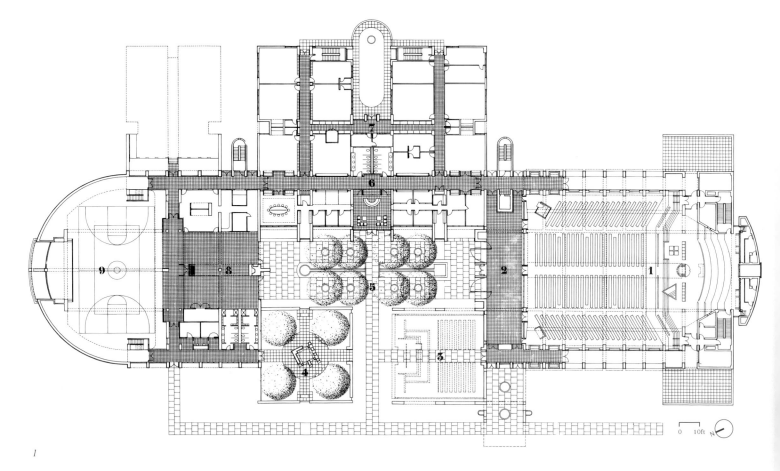

1

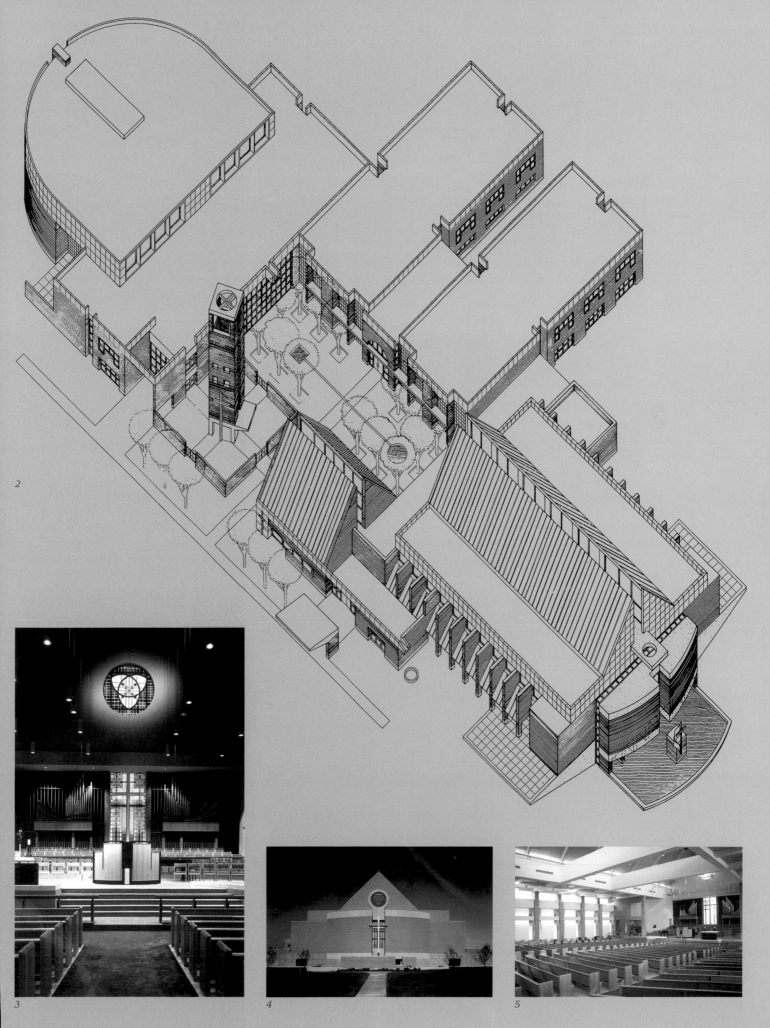

2

3

4

5

St. Stephen's Catholic Church

Warwick, New York, USA

St. Stephen's Catholic Church, designed by Bentel & Bentel Architects, is located on a verdant site set in the rolling farmland of Orange County, outside of downtown Warwick where it had been based for many years. The natural characteristics of the property—namely an impressive 'plantation' of red pines and an even more impressive though less formal group of ancient maple and oak trees—were used as integral parts of the site design. An existing school and convent were also drawn into the overall composition to serve, with the new church complex, as the boundaries of a series of outdoor courtyards.

The internal organization of the church reflects the recent thinking about Catholic church design outlined in *Environment and Art in Catholic Worship*. The liturgical consultant was Fr Richard Vosko. The large atrium serves as a secular gathering room that can accommodate 100 congregants comfortably under the raised roof of the assembly area. The main sanctuary, which can seat 650 to 700 worshipers, takes its inspiration from two sources. While its overall shape recalls many of the larger rural buildings in the region, the structural steel columns and bracketing in the sanctuary reiterate the form of the pines. Alternatively, these steel trees also suggest the ribs of Gothic stone vaulting or the outstretched arms of Christ on the cross.

The sacristies and the parish center/rectory are each given their own character and scale in order to make these programmatic element legible on the exterior and interior. By composing these separate elements of the program informally, as a kind of ecclesiastical village, the design of the new church acknowledges both the overall form and massing of the vernacular farm complexes that are integral to the identity of the region.

1

2

3

1   The sanctuary is a wide, generous space where
    all the seats have close proximity to the altar
2   Illumination highlights the use of natural
    materials in the sanctuary
3   Section BB
4   South elevation
5   East elevation
6   Site plan
7   The altar is found on a wall of glass, which
    views out to the woods beyond
Photography: Eduard Hueber, Arch Photo, Inc.

SEA RANCH CHAPEL

Sea Ranch, California, USA

This chapel is very small—only about 360 square feet—but its form and its materials have an other-worldly character befitting a work of art. The Sea Ranch Chapel was actually designed by an artist, James T. Hubbell, for a spectacular site overlooking the Pacific Ocean. Visible from an adjacent highway to beckon passers-by to visit, the arresting forms create a space that is dark and mysterious, a grotto-like environment that connects one with the organic elements.

The chapel is the gift of Robert and Betty Buffman, who donated it to the memory of a friend, Kirk Ditzler—a naturalist and artist. To design a chapel in the spirit of the man it is dedicated to, Hubbell studied Ditzler's drawings of the area's flora and fauna. Look at the chapel design and you see suggestions of sea animals, rock outcroppings, native plants. The chapel appears to grow from the very site upon which it rests, expressing the elements of the world around it.

Except for some engineering drawings required to show how the chapel would be supported, there were no working drawings for the chapel. Hubbell produced a teak wood scale model with a removable roof to guide the builders in their work. The model would become the reference point used to shape the chapel's wood roofs and rustic stone walls. Selecting a contractor who had been trained in Japan in the art of temple and boat building (a perfect union of craft that the design demanded), Hubbell collaborated with the builders to determine in the field how the chapel would be framed and finished.

The result is a building in constant motion, moving as you move around it, whose floating roofs admit slices of stained-glass-colored light, washing wood, stone, and ceramic surfaces. While the exterior form may summon the visitor from afar, it is the temple's intimate interior that elevates materials to a sacrament of craft.

1 Plan
2 Concept sketch
3 The chapel's organic forms are at home in this natural setting
4 The chapel's roof arcs to the sky, creating a link between the spiritual and craftsmanship
5 Building forms suggest the organic life forms found in the sketches of an amateur naturalist
6 The entry doors lead to a narrow passage to the chapel's inner sanctum
7 Chapel interior employs the same natural, rustic materials as the exterior
Photography: Alan Weintraub

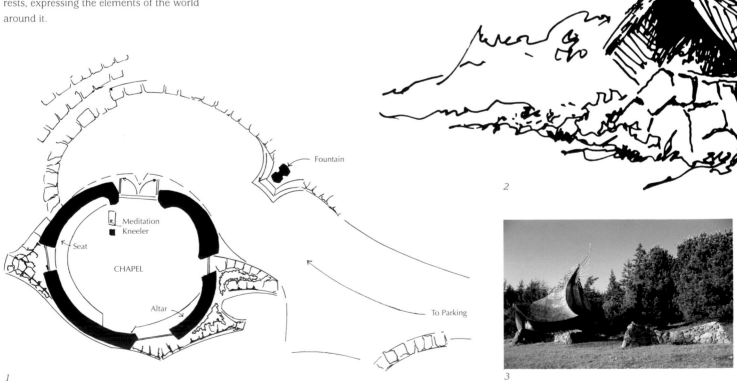

Fountain

Meditation
Kneeler

Seat

CHAPEL

Altar

To Parking

1

2

3

4

5

7

6

BROWN MEMORIAL WOODBROOK PRESBYTERIAN CHURCH

Baltimore, Maryland, USA

The two existing buildings on the seven-acre site had been built in 1960. The originally designed sanctuary was never built however, and the congregation had been worshipping in the fellowship hall for over 30 years. It was the desire of the church to build a new sanctuary not only to accommodate a growing congregation, but also to upgrade their facility for handicapped accessibility and oil energy efficiency, and to increase their visibility along an adjacent major thoroughfare.

Ziger/Snead, Inc. Architects responded with a design for a new sanctuary with organ, narthex, tower, connecting walkway, interior renovations and landscape master plan. The new sanctuary is designed both to respect the relatively quiet nature of the existing modern buildings, and to create a dramatic and sculptural focus for the entire facility which reaches out to the community.

The architectural concept for the church consists of the relationship between its two main elements—body and roof. The body of the church is a massive, hand-crafted, square brick box. The roof is a delicate, hovering, wood and steel barrel vault, rotated and tilted over the box below. These two elements create a dialogue between the rational and the spiritual, the earth and the sky, knowledge and faith.

Within the sanctuary, curving oak pews, radiating aisles, and the roof form reinforce the raised chancel area as the focus of community worship. The chancel is located in the corner of the square space, creating a dynamic yet intimate quality. The Holtcamp organ provides both a focus and backdrop for the activities of the church. In its role as central focus, it is designed as a free-standing modern sculptural element within the sanctuary enclosure. Its dramatically sweeping pipes reinforce the central axis of the church,

and echo the lines of the roof, pews, and chancel. The organ also responds to its role as a backdrop for worship in its concave shape, open center, and understated detail.

The floors are slate, the walls are Norwegian brick, and the ceiling is a light-colored wood deck with curved and tapered steel beams. Theatrical lighting illuminates the chancel while small fixtures hover over the congregation, reinforcing the vault of the roof.

1

2

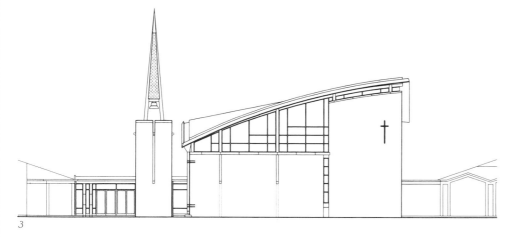
3

1   *View from the north shows how new architecture works with old*
2   *From the southeast, the tower marks the entry to the sanctuary*
3   *Elevation*
4   *Site plan*

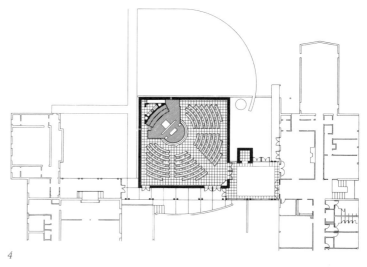
4

5   The curved roof form creates a sense
    of dynamism
Opposite:
    Organ dominates the sanctuary interior
Photography: Neil Meyerhoff (1,2);
Alan Karchmer (5,6)

5

METROPOLITAN CATHEDRAL OF MANAGUA

Managua, Nicaragua

In 1972, an earthquake destroyed Managua's Catholic Cathedral. This new cathedral designed by Legorreta Arquitectos, is located in the upper part of the city on a site of 29 acres. It not only replaces the old cathedral but has become the new center of Managua. Under the decisive promotion and support of Thomas Monahan, the leadership of a devoted Cardinal, and the hope of a faithful congregation, the Cathedral has become much more than a building—the symbol of faith of a suffering country.

The design responds to the notion that contemporary Catholic congregations have moved from a passive role to one of participation with ecclesiastic authorities. The close proximity and architectural integration of the altar with the congregants express this relationship. For the same reasons, the highest of the cathedral's 63 domes is located at the center of the congregation. The design gives the solemnity that the cathedral needs without monumentality or ostentation.

The cathedral is versatile in accommodating the various functions of the liturgical year. Two or three times annually the Cardinal celebrates Mass from the exterior altar that sits above the main door, to large congregations of approximately 100,000 who gather in the esplanade. Periodic ceremonies take place in the main nave 150 feet long by 40 feet wide, with a capacity of 1,000 people. The daily Mass is celebrated in the Santisimo Chapel, which is 1,700 square feet. Finally, the venerated image of the Sangre de Cristo is located in a dedicated circular chapel 40 feet in diameter. Because of its shape and illumination, candle light and color are an adequate frame for spiritual gatherings.

The cathedral's chiseled concrete responds to the raw spirituality and bravery of the country. The floor is designed as a colored carpet of geometric forms and is of hand-made concrete tiles. Doors and benches are of native wood. The domes provide natural light and ventilation. In total, the building represents the culture and climate of Nicaragua, and pays homage to the people who have suffered deeply but maintain their faith and courage.

1

2

1 The ethereal Chapel of Veneration allows
  worship of the Eucharist
2 The cathedral rises above the landscape of
  the countryside
3 Interior view of the main entry doors to
  the cathedral worship space
4 The cathedral's main worship space combines
  color, natural light, and tactile materials
5 View of cathedral worship space towards
  the main altar.
6 Detail of lights in main worship space,
  suggest crosses

Photography: Lourdes Legorreta (1,2,3,4,6);
Peter Aaron (5)

4

5

6

3

ROCK CHURCH

Killingworth, Connecticut, USA

Located in the rural town of Killingworth, Connecticut, Rock Church was designed by Dennis J. Dowd and constructed, for the most part, by members of the small congregation.

Rock Church is sited at the culmination of the entry drive and provides a strong presence when viewed from the county road. From this approach, the church appears to be a large, elegantly detailed barn, a form not only appropriate for its rural setting, but also referential to the birthplace of the Christ child.

The layering of internal volumes, alternating from low intimate spaces to more majestic high spaces, separated by a series of similarly fenestrated walls, reinforces the entrance sequence begun at the entry drive and ending at the sanctuary altar and baptismal font. The backdrop wall at the rear of the altar is visually reminiscent of the front facade.

Continued

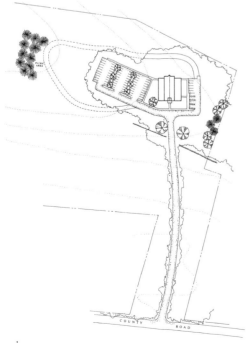

1

2

3

4

1 Site plan
2 Rendering
3 Church is approached by a rural drive
4 Front facade is symmetrical and barn-like

The 10,000-square-foot floor plan is organized by using support spaces to insulate and protect the sanctuary space. The open roof structure gives the sanctuary a sense of scale and articulation. In keeping with the budget, materials throughout are simple: wood trusses, drywall, carpet, tile, and wood siding.

The goal of the congregation was to work within its modest budget without compromising aspirations for a spiritually uplifting place of worship. Rock Church was designed for later expansion and changes in use. For example, expansion of the sanctuary is achieved by locating non-bearing partitions between the sanctuary and temporary classrooms. These partitions can be removed to expand this space. All issues of code compliance, as well as technical aspects such as flooring, ceilings, and detail continuity, have been considered from the initial design. This will allow the sanctuary expansion to occur with minimal disruption. Future permanent classrooms will be added to the west side of the building with a continuation of the existing low roof wrapping around the west side in a hip roof design.

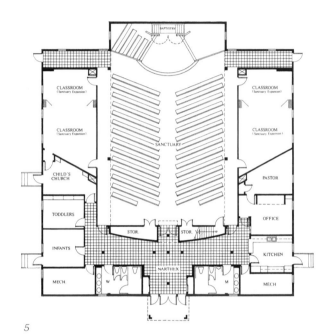

5

6

5   Floor plan
6   Roof structure gives the sanctuary scale.
7   Section
8   Narthex ceiling has an open structure
9   Sanctuary wall is punctuated with a loft
Photography: Robert Benson

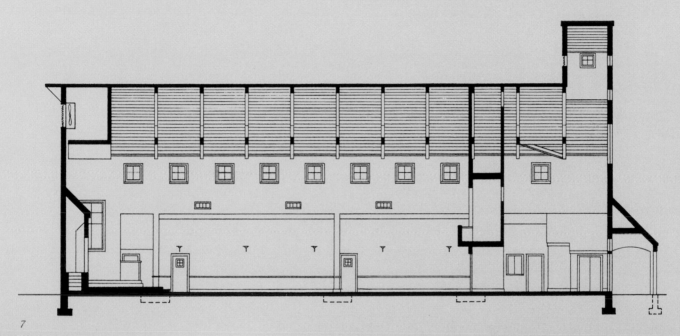

7

8

9

AGUDAS ACHIM SYNAGOGUE

San Antonio, Texas, USA

Agudas Achim Synagogue is a 44,000-square-foot facility that includes a sanctuary that can accommodate 800, a large social hall, a library, classrooms, offices, and a 115-seat chapel. Designed by Finegold Alexander + Associates, this synagogue is at once contemporary and regional. The exterior cladding of stucco is in the spirit of adobe construction, while the muted exterior colors of brown, beige, purple, and yellow capture the hues found in the region's desert flora. The colors also help to break up the mass of the building, making it more intelligible.

The building is embraced by a protective wall, which opens at the front with large cedar doors that recall the entrance to a Spanish mission compound. The entry sequence allows one to pass from the secular world to that of the sacred. Such a sequence of passage continues inside the building, where one is delivered to a light-filled foyer dominated by an octagonal rotunda that gives one a clear sense that they have arrived.

One then passes through a vestibule to the sanctuary—a large space with balcony seating—that can be intimate as well. A hallmark of the sanctuary is its judicious use of natural light. Clear side windows under the balconies look out onto deciduous trees that filter the sunlight. The focus of the sanctuary is its back wall behind the bimah, which is rendered in a rough native limestone. This makes a connection to the Western Wall in Jerusalem. The stone's texture is further enhanced by the narrow slit windows that frame it and visually hold it off from the barrel vaulted roof and the side walls. Raked with this band of light, the wall seems heavier and more ancient. The imposing ark doors are inscribed with the Ten Commandments, which disappear behind an abstract scroll work that brings to mind several images—the open pages of a book, a gathering of worshipers, or the parting waves of the Red Sea.

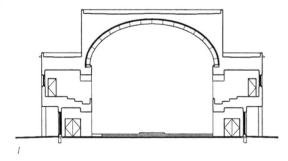

1   Section through sanctuary
2   Section through library
3   Chapel glows at night, revealing its intimate seating arrangement
4   Section through community and entry court

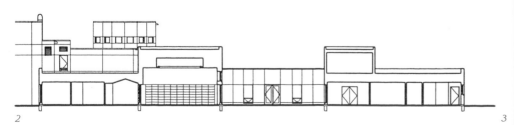

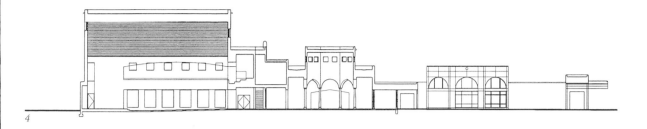

4

Opposite:
Walk leading from gated entry to the sanctuary,
with chapel wing at right

6   *Floor plan*

7   *The synagogue complex is entered through*
heavy wooden doors that lead to a protected
courtyard

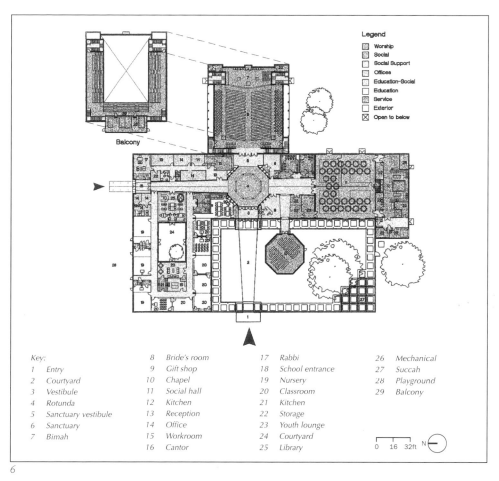

Balcony

Legend

- Worship
- Social
- Social Support
- Offices
- Education-Social
- Education
- Service
- Exterior
- Open to below

Key:

1	Entry	8	Bride's room	17	Rabbi
2	Courtyard	9	Gift shop	18	School entrance
3	Vestibule	10	Chapel	19	Nursery
4	Rotunda	11	Social hall	20	Classroom
5	Sanctuary vestibule	12	Kitchen	21	Kitchen
6	Sanctuary	13	Reception	22	Storage
7	Bimah	14	Office	23	Youth lounge
		15	Workroom	24	Courtyard
		16	Cantor	25	Library

26	Mechanical
27	Succah
28	Playground
29	Balcony

0   16   32ft   N

6

7

7 *View from sanctuary through rotunda to the*
   main entry doors
Opposite:
   Sanctuary is dominated by a wall of rough
   native limestone
Photography: Peter Vanderwarker

7

CHRIST CHURCH, LAKE FOREST

Lake Forest, Illinois, USA

The Lake Forest Congregational Church began planning its expansion within five years of its founding in 1980. The congregation was given a 10-acre site on the edge of town, and began to develop a master plan. The design, by Hammel Green and Abrahamson, evolved after careful study of the New England village—the birthplace of the Congregational Church. At the center of the complex is a serene garden courtyard defined by Puritan style buildings around the perimeter. The master plan calls for a 1,000-seat meeting house and four smaller 'houses' for religious education, social functions, and church offices. The buildings take the classic form of Colonial New England buildings: simple, rectangular flat elevations, gable roofs, dormers, rectangular windows with divided lights, crisp detailing, and no color. The village concept embodies the formal symmetry and simplicity of the congregation's Puritan heritage.

Phase one of the construction includes the meeting house, the bell tower, and one of the four houses that flank the courtyard. Visitors enter the meeting house through the bell tower, which serves as the focal point for the entire complex. The tower is detached from the church itself and leads to a glassy narthex. This narthex space connects the meeting house to the ancillary building. In the warm months of the year, the balcony on the bell tower serves as a pulpit for outdoor services in the courtyard.

The interior of the meeting house reflects the same simplicity of form and materials as the exterior. Like its New England antecedents, the meeting house is a buoyant, light-filled volume. Luminous white walls and warm-toned woodwork accentuate the elegant symmetry of the basic geometric forms so characteristic of Puritan architectural expression.

1   Church exterior architecture is inspired by
    the denomination's Puritan roots
2   Entry to the complex of connected buildings
    is gained through the tower

1

2

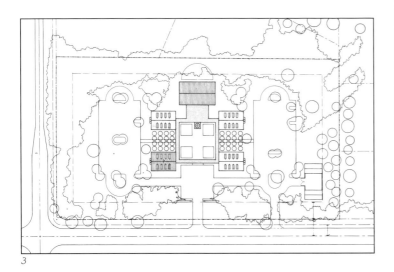

3

4

5

3   Site plan
4   Interior is simple in its use of unadorned white walls
5   The spare, but uplifting interior is inspired by those of New England
     meeting houses
Photography: Jess Smith/PHOTOSMITH

CHAPEL OF ST. IGNATIUS

Seattle, Washington, USA

1

2

3

Seattle University, a Jesuit school of about 6,000 students, is the setting for a new chapel designed by Steven Holl—Olson/Sundberg was the Associate Architect. Holl met with students and faculty while generating the design concept. He also visited the European sites of the mission of St. Ignatius of Loyola, founder of the Jesuit order. In his writings St. Ignatius is noted for viewing spiritual life as a balance of consolations and desolations, or lights and darks. Holl conceived of the chapel as 'a box containing seven bottles of light.' The 'bottles' are expressed on the exterior as figural light scoops. Different qualities of light are found throughout the cavernous chapel interior: natural sunlight at the procession and narthex; yellow light in combination with a blue window (and vice versa) in the nave; orange light in combination with a purple window at the chapel of the Blessed Sacrament; green light in combination with a red window at the choir stall; purple light in combination with an orange window in the confessional. On the exterior, projecting and reflected light are found in the forecourt and pool. Natural light on the interior is ever-changing, and is alive as it strikes the curved plaster walls, which are rendered with a rough texture. In contrast, the highly polished dark-tinted concrete floor reflects light. Artificial light is provided through fluorescent lamps which light the concealed recessed walls, allowing the glowing color effects to be visible at night. Throughout the sanctuary are hanging pendants of clear, irregularly blown glass that appear to be inverted chalices or votive candles, conjuring images that are part of the Catholic tradition. Holl also designed the wall sconces of bubbled glass. The artificial lights can be preset at different intensities for different types of liturgical events.

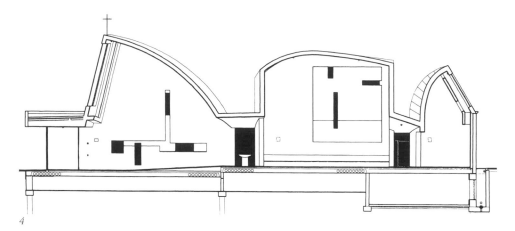

4

5

7

1 Raking light reveals texture of hand-troweled plaster work
2 Light emits from behind a wall with an eerie glow
3 Contrasting colors are used in the contemporary stained glass
4 Section reveals the diversity of space geometry
5 The chapel as viewed across the reflecting pool
6 Throughout the chapel are hand-made art pieces of glass.
7 View through the sanctuary toward a side chapel
Photography: Solange Fabiáo

6

ST. PETER'S LUTHERAN CHURCH

Columbus, Indiana, USA

The architectural concept for this church, designed by Gunnar Birkerts and Associates, incorporates and expresses the many traditional qualities of the congregation and the many architectural qualities of Lutheran religious architecture. This church adopts these qualities for today and projects them into the future.

As we congregate and seek togetherness, our bodies tend to group in a circle. As we worship we are seeking direction. This direction is given to us by turning towards the religious symbol or the spoken word. Togetherness and direction are the basis of the plan for this church. As much as the seating and the symmetry of worship is expressive of the spiritual side of the church, the

reality of the daily world is expressed by the form development of the enclosing space. The left and the right, the day and the night, the north and the south, the circle and the square are all present in the interior space. The exterior form is also faithful to these interior considerations. This house of God is topped by a spire celebrating its presence in the larger community and announcing its allegiance to earlier Lutheran church forms with their predominant spires establishing their religious affiliation.

The copper-clad spire is terminated by a gold cross supported by a gold sphere following the European tradition of early Lutheran churches.

The primary materials for the exterior of the church are brick and concrete. The concrete is used to bring structural and also visual stability to the exterior walls. Brick, used as infill, continues the local building tradition. All three exterior materials—concrete, brick, and copper—are woven into an architectural pattern of forms, planes, and textures.

On the interior the walls and ceiling of the sanctuary space are lightly textured, white painted, gypsum wall board. The floor finish is sealed concrete with carpet in the aisles and at the chancel space. The liturgical furniture, pews, base and handrails are maple. An 18-foot diameter chandelier lights the sanctuary space.

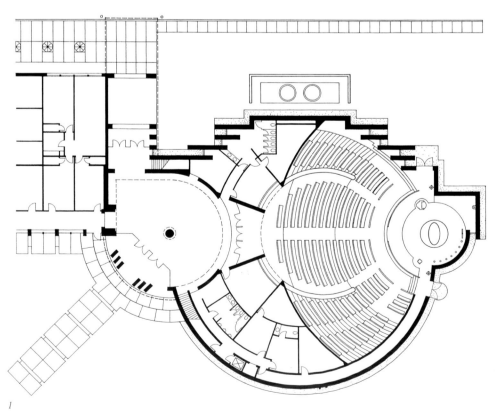

1

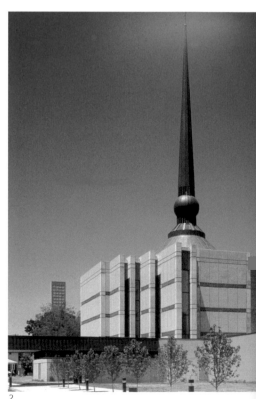

2

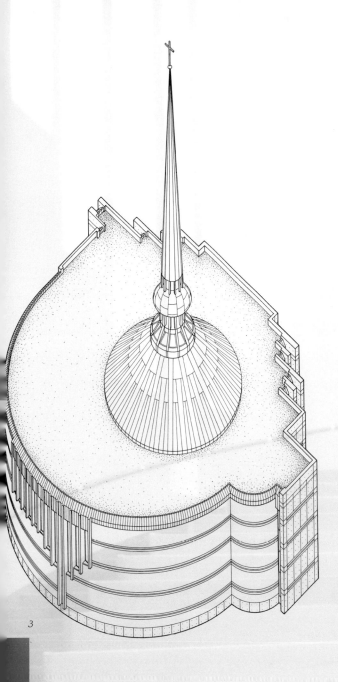

3

1. *Floor plan*
2. *Entrance side to the church, as it faces the parking lot*
3. *Axonometric roof plan*
4. *Sanctuary's seating arrangement allows an intimate gathering in the round*
5. *Oculus over the sanctuary suggests the domes of traditional churches*
6. *Church from the eastern approach, creates a landmark on the skyline*
7. *Woodwork suggests the fenestration pattern of the church exterior*
8. *Long windows allow even, northern light into the sanctuary*

Photography: courtesy Gunnar Birkerts

5

6

4

7

8

WILLIAMS COLLEGE
JEWISH RELIGIOUS CENTER

Williamstown, Massachusetts, USA

1

T his Jewish Religious Center is next to a neighborhood of large, 19ᵗʰ century and early 20ᵗʰ century homes. The center attempts to conform to this context while at the same time expressing a certain monumentality. Participation in the ritual by congregants sharing a common experience is critical to the Jewish liturgy. Therefore, eye contact among congregants is desirable. Jewish religious ritual calls for a literate congregation requiring space illuminated for reading.

Herbert S. Newman & Partners' design concept for the building is based on a reflection of the way Jewish religious buildings have evolved. Since the Jewish ritual does not prescribe any particular architectural form or style of building, their forms over the millennia have typically adapted traditional regional styles to the functional and ritual requirements of each congregation. Following in the tradition of vernacular New England architecture, the Jewish

2

3

4

5

1   The center fronts the street with a domestic
    scale
2   The white exterior is an arrangement
    of complex forms
3   Normal seating
4&5 Expanded seating
6   Expanded seating plan
Photography: Steve Rosenthal

Religious Center is a wooden building painted
white inside and out and given monumental
scale by a dominant vertical element.

The new building contains a sanctuary, a dining
room (with two Kosher kitchens) and a library.
These rooms are contiguous and can be used by
300 people during high holy days. The flexibility
to accommodate these numbers is achieved by
opening the dining room and library to the
central space. The expanded seating
arrangement enables all the congregants to have
a close relationship with the reader and with
each other. Locating the bimah in the center of
the congregation allows the service to be
conducted with the reader or rabbi in the middle
of the space.

This building, which won an award from the
Interfaith Forum on Religion, Art, and
Architecture was praised by the awards jury.
"The general shape attracts and invites. The
interior seems consistent with Jewish liturgy,
including the expanded plan for high holy days.
The exterior is original and has a definite New
England character."

6

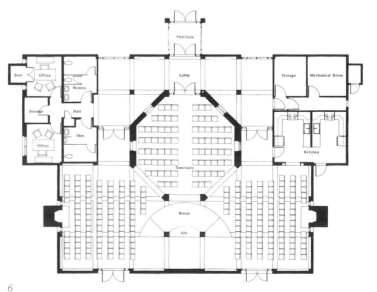

CHURCH OF THE NATIVITY

Rancho Santa Fe, California, USA

In a rural valley north of La Jolla, the client for this church wanted to establish, as did the early California missionaries, a parish around which a Christian community would develop. Designed by Moore Ruble Yudell Architects, the buildings of the Church of the Nativity form a walled compound, set back from the road to create a sense of a place apart from, yet open to, the community. A dirt road on axis with the church building leads through a grove of trees to the main cloister. This notion of a protected cloister is also commonly found in the early missions.

Within the walls, the church building, parish hall, four chapels, and columbarium, in Spanish-American tradition, are oriented inward. Their placement creates a series of cloisters and gardens, layered to establish a sequence of spaces that culminates in the place of worship. One enters the protective courtyard through a gate, which is found in the long stuccoed cloister wall between the library and administration wings. The cloister is a combination of paved surfaces and gardens, providing space for church community gatherings. Dominating the courtyard space is the church's tower, which rises high above the cloister to mark the church on the skyline (as is common with the older missions).

The church sanctuary has a longitudinal nave with a single transept. This arrangement offers semi-circular seating for up to 550 congregants. Seating fans out from the altar, engendering a strong sense of community and proximity to the celebrants. The altar wall intersects the crossing, while large openings at its two ends wash the walls with indirect natural light. Ambulatories, aisles, shrines, and color evoke ecclesiastical architectural tradition, separated from the nave by columns and screens.

Future plans call for a school site behind the church compound and linked to it by porches, gardens, and courts.

1

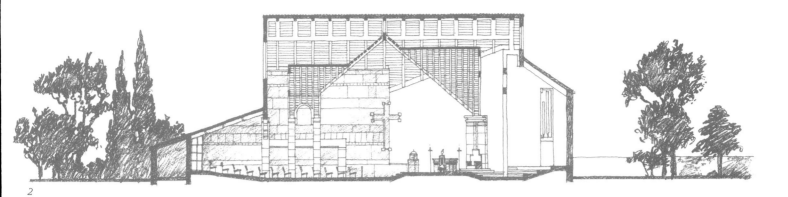

2

3

1   *Within the cloister, the tower marks the entry*
     to the narthex and the church

2   *Section*

3   *From the cloister, one enters the narthex with*
     the baptismal font at the center

4   Site plan
5   View from the covered walkway of the cloister
    toward the entry of the chapel
Opposite:
    This large space has a sense of intimacy from
    the altar table, as pews fan around it
Following pages:
    The main aisle to the sanctuary is on a diagonal
    to accentuate the space
Photography: Timothy Hursley

4

5

FAITH LUTHERAN CHURCH

Clive, Iowa, USA

A congregation housed in a prototype mission church at the edge of a rapidly growing suburban community merged with another congregation. The congregation needed to expand the existing church to include a 500-person sanctuary, a large fellowship hall, classrooms, and specialty rooms. They also expressed an interest in using the 4,800-square-foot existing building and parking lot in an effort to make their tight budget go as far as possible. The new church of 19,000 square feet was designed by Herbert Lewis Kruse Blunck Architecture.

The setting afforded two different contexts in which to generate an architectural response: an agricultural complex across the prairie, and a community gathering at the base of the church on the mount. A neutral palette of materials is used throughout, left in their natural state.

The existing sanctuary is virtually swallowed up by the new construction to become the central commons and narthex for the new complex. The baptismal font is centered on the space to signify both the rebirth and the origin of the church and building. The font becomes the biaxial focus for the new cruciform plan, around which the entire church revolves.

The square cruciform plan of the sanctuary allows the 'gathering of the family' around the altar. The broad seating area generates a space that recalls a meeting hall. A glass clerestory arising over the altar acknowledges its liturgical significance, reinforces the major axis connecting all four elements of worship, and fills this space with an ethereal light. The prow of the church, at the terminus of the sanctuary, suggests a ship sailing across the open prairie. An open bell tower marks the new east entrance.

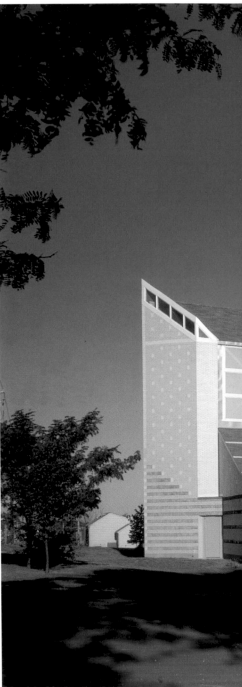

1

2

1 From a distance, the church complex appears
   as an assemblage of smaller buildings
2 From the southeast, the church has the
   presence of a ship, with its prow southward
3 Section

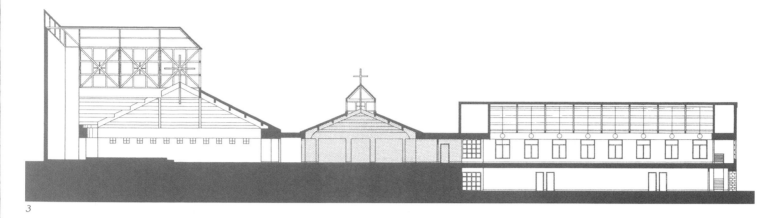

3

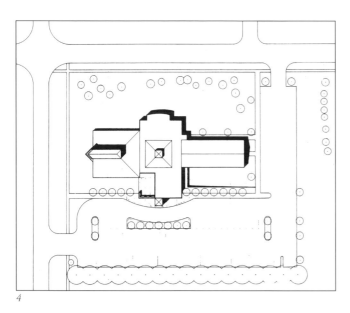

4

4 Site plan
5 The south end of the church suggests an abstracted image of
   a traditional steeple
6 Detail of the church's 'prow,' with its decorative brick pattern

5

6

7 The sanctuary is filled with natural light,
   delivered by a mammoth clerestory over the
   altar table
Right:
   The narthex or commons area surrounds
   a baptismal font, with the sanctuary beyond
Photography: Assassi Productions

7

MARILYN MOYER MEDITATION CHAPEL

Portland, Oregon, USA

Seeking a small, enduring, yet striking structure, the program for this chapel was simple: provide a non-denominational public building for thought and meditation that will offer solace to those seeking it; a place to read, or write a letter; design a building that is overtly religious by virtue of its location and art work, yet more subtly conveys the spiritual in its approach and form.

The project, designed by Thompson Vaivoda & Associates, occupies the most visually prominent location of a 58-acre suburban Catholic sanctuary. Perched atop a nearly vertical basalt cliff, 130 feet high, the specific building site selected offers panoramic views from the urban center to the mountainous wilderness. The trees and land forms are an integral part of the approach to the building.

A major plaza serves as a hub, offering directions to the various features and facilities of the upper level. The path to the chapel follows an existing trail through the woods with large rock formations to both sides that intermittently offers glimpses of the building through the flora. The path terminates in a small elevated plaza that prepares and orients the visitor.

Entering the chapel, the visitor experiences a dramatic view to the north as the bent glass wall rises 28 feet, interrupted only by a 'mother and child' sculpture placed on axis with the entry. Fixed furniture occurs as pew benches to each side of the entrance and along the sides. Seating areas are raised slightly to offer an element of privacy while movable seating can be used to augment capacity for a wedding or other larger gatherings. Two small decks terminate the perimeter bench seating for those seeking a writing surface, yet still maintaining the view. The large chord forms a wall plane that supports a simple steel bar joist roof. The floor slab is supported by a precast concrete beam and single column forming a cross whose base rests on a platform incised in the rock wall.

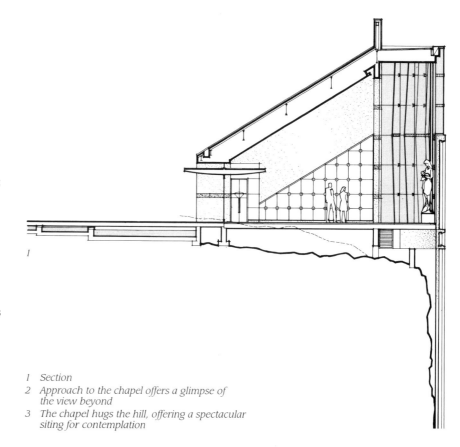

1

1   Section
2   Approach to the chapel offers a glimpse of
    the view beyond
3   The chapel hugs the hill, offering a spectacular
    siting for contemplation

2   3

4

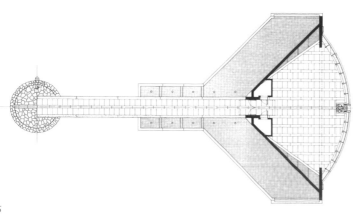

5

6

7

4   The building form folds over a moat that fronts the chapel
5   Plan
6   The entrance reads as a bridge, spanning over space to deliver
     one to the chapel's heart
7   Chapel interior is elegant in its simplicity, as seen in the glazed south wall
Following pages:
     The city spreads out below the quiet solitude of the chapel
Photography: Richard Strode, Strode Eckert Photographic

Author and Contributor Notes

Michael J. Crosbie, Ph.D., is an architect, author, journalist, and teacher. A former editor of *Progressive Architecture*, he is the author of numerous books on architecture. Dr. Crosbie has written for a number of journals and magazines, including *Historic Preservation*, *Domus*, *Architectural Record*, and *Landscape Architecture*, and has won several journalism awards. He is currently the assistant editor of *Faith & Form* magazine. He teaches architecture at Roger Williams University, and has lectured at architecture schools in North America and abroad. Dr. Crosbie practices with Steven Winter Associates, an architectural research and consulting firm in Norwalk, Connecticut, and lives with his family in Essex, Connecticut.

Fr. Richard S. Vosko, Ph.D., is the 1994 recipient of the inter-faith Elbert M. Conover Award for his contributions to religious art and architecture. Many of his projects have received recognition for liturgical and design excellence. A priest of the Diocese of Albany, New York, Fr. Vosko has worked throughout the United States and Canada as a designer and consultant for worship environments since 1970. He served as liturgical designer on a number of projects in this book, including St. James Cathedral, St. Stephen's Church, and St. Thomas More Church.

ACKNOWLEDGMENTS

Michael J. Crosbie

I would like to express my thanks to the people who made this book possible: to Paul Latham, Alessina Brooks, and their staff at The Images Publishing Group Pty Ltd; to the architects and designers who have allowed their work to appear in this volume, and who supplied materials and insight for their documentation; to the dozens of photographers who generously gave permission for the use of the photographs; to my colleagues at the Interfaith Forum for Religious Art and Architecture and at *Faith & Form* magazine who suggested outstanding religious buildings for inclusion; to Fr. Richard S. Vosko, liturgical designer and consultant, for his illuminating Introduction; and, finally, to those congregations who raised the funds, organized the building committees, and saw their projects through to completion, with courage and commitment.